THE COMPLETE GUIDE TO

I DRESSAGE

THE COMPLETE GUIDE TO DRESSAGE

■

JENNIE LORISTON-CLARKE

Ebury Press
Horizons

A QUARTO BOOK

Ebury Press Limited

An imprint of Random Century Ltd
20 Vauxhall Bridge Road,
London SW1V 2SA

Random Century Australia (Pty) Ltd
20 Alfred Street,
Milsons Point, NSW 2061

Random Century New Zealand Limited
32-34 View Road, PO Box 60-086, Glenfield,
Auckland 10

Random Century South Africa (Pty) Ltd
PO Box 337, Bergviei 2012, South Africa

This paperback edition first published in 1989
by Stanley Paula & Co Ltd

Reprinted 1995

British Library Cataloguing in Publication Data
Loriston-Clarise, Jennie
  The complete guide to dressage
  1. Dressage
  I. Title
  798.2'3   SF309.5

ISBN 0-09-174430-X

This book was designed and produced by
Quarto Publishing plc
The Old Brewery
6 Blundell Street
London N7 9BH

Senior editor Helen Owen
Art Editor Ursula Dawson

Editors Anne Selby, Sally Taylor
Designer Robin Mitchell
Illustrator Craig Austin

Art director Moira Clinch
Editorial Director Carolyn King

Typeset by Text Filmsetter Ltd and Comproom Ltd.
Manufactured in Hong Kong by Regent Publishing Services Ltd
Printed by Leefung-Asco Printers Ltd, China

CONTENTS

FOREWORD

Dressage is, perhaps, the most fascinating of horse sports. Its very name may seem strange to some people but really it means simply 'to dress' or 'to train'. What this actually entails is the training of a noble, responsive, trusting animal to carry himself in the best possible way. In dressage, he learns to perform all his natural paces correctly and under the control of the rider.

The horse, for me and for many others, is the most beautiful of God's domesticated animals. He is really a herd creature but is, nevertheless, readily prepared to live in a stable and take up the companionship of man. Like most animals, he likes some form of discipline and is keen to please his master. I have studied horses from childhood, and their breeding and training has captivated me ever since. In this book, I hope to convey how a horse learns and behaves, how he understands and reacts to his rider's demands – because dressage is a partnership between horse and rider, and the rider who does not study his horse's character, or who treats him like a machine, is the one least likely to succeed.

Jennie Loriston-Clarke.

Dressage is an exacting sport which requires perfect understanding and co-operation between horse and rider. When this is achieved through years of patient training, beautiful, flowing movements, such as this **extended trot,** look deceptively easy.

CHAPTER ONE

THE
STORY OF DRESSAGE

INTRODUCTION

DRESSAGE: A CONSUMING INTEREST

THE ORIGINS OF DRESSAGE

THE IMPERIAL SPANISH RIDING SCHOOL

HORSEMEN WHO MADE HISTORY

Officers of the **Cadre Noir,** the cavalry school in Saumur, France, have
long been exponents of the art of dressage. Horses and riders are
trained in all aspects of dressage, culminating in the 'airs off the ground'.
These spectacular movements, some of which were once used in
battle, are now seen only in special displays.

DRESSAGE: A CONSUMING INTEREST

I have had a consuming interest in dressage ever since I watched Helsinki Olympic Silver Medallist Madame Liz Hartel give a display at the Horse of the Year Show in London in 1952. Riding her mare Jubilee, Madame Hartel gave a memorable display of elegance, freedom and ease of movement to music, which I have tried to emulate throughout my career.

It was twelve years before I managed to win my first Prix St George Test, riding the lovely but temperamental Anglo-Arab mare Desert Storm. This mare taught me a tremendous amount, and would no doubt have been an even better horse, had I known more myself. The Thoroughbred stallion Xenocles gave me a lot more experience when I acquired him as a four-year-old racehorse and trained him to become an Advanced Event horse and a Grand Prix Dressage horse. He also bred me some lovely foals, and his grandson Catherston Dancing Storm looked a born champion when only two days old.

I then had a ride on Mrs Gill Steele's Kadett which gave me the opportunities I had dreamed of, to represent Britain in the Olympic Games, first at Munich in 1972, and then at Montreal in 1976. Kadett, a beautiful Thoroughbred/Trakehner cross, a nervous but elegant animal, gave me many heartaches and many wonderful moments as well. He performed some sensational displays in his time, and gave me my first international success at Fontainebleau, when we won the Kur Free Style Test in 1975.

In 1972 Mrs Steele and I bought a three-year-old Thoroughbred Dutch stallion from Holland, and called him Dutch Courage. Within a few years I realized I had a star performer — the ease with which he learned, his balance and his suppleness made everything seem effortless. In 1978 he won an Individual Bronze Medal in the World Championships held in Britain in the beautiful grounds of Goodwood House, Sussex. In 1980 he proceeded to win every class he entered in the Inchcape International Championships at Goodwood. From that year too he was consistently in the top six places in the World, European and Alternative Olympic

Dutch Gold competing at Goodwood. This quality horse, sired by Dutch Courage, has proved himself versatile enough to win eventing and show jumping competitions, as well as becoming a Grand Prix dressage horse.

Dutch Courage at Goodwood in 1981. It is perhaps with this horse that I have enjoyed the greatest partnership. He came to me in 1972, and in 1974 I realized he was the most promising horse I had ever had to train. His intelligence, generosity and amazing suppleness enabled him to become an international dressage horse at a very young age.

Championships. And he never failed to capture the hearts of all those who watched him perform.

Dutch Courage sired a champion line of dressage competition horses. Both of his sons, Catherston Dutch Bid and Dutch Gold, show every sign of following in their father's footsteps. Dutch Gold is my present Grand Prix horse, and is one of the horses shown in the photographs throughout this book; the others are Catherston Dutch Bid and Dutch Courage.

In 1986 Dutch Gold and I came a close third in the Musical Freestyle event of the World Championships in Toronto. I shall be looking at the international dressage competitions of recent years in greater detail in the concluding chapter of this book. But first, what are the origins of dressage — this art form of horse riding, which has captured the imaginations of riders all over the world?

Sidesaddle dressage When a horse is correctly and thoroughly trained, it may be ridden sidesaddle as successfully as astride. The high level of training compensates for the lack of leg aids, and the horse learns to respond to the seat just as easily. Here, I am giving a sidesaddle dressage display at the Olympia Horse Show on Kadett.

MAN AND HORSE

Horses and horsemanship have been part of man's history for centuries: it is difficult to know exactly when the horse was first ridden. A relief on the tomb of the Pharaoh Horemheb of Egypt shows a rider sitting on the rump of a horse in about 1600 BC, but it was several hundred years more before any real form of horsemanship was shown.

The horse was certainly used in the valleys of ancient Syria and Egypt and on the flat lands around the Tigris and Euphrates. Because the horses there were only about 13 to 14 hands in height, however, they were employed mostly to pull wheeled vehicles. These horses were hardly large enough to carry a rider. In the mountains of southern Asia, where the men were smaller, the stocky hill ponies of northern India and the Himalayan regions have not changed much over the centuries: they are tough, strong, hardy beasts and extremely sure-footed.

In about 1300 BC the horse was used extensively to pull chariots. When the Hyksos broke out of Asia Minor into the Near East the horses became larger through cross-breeding, and were then used more as riding horses. At this time the first horseman's manual was written by the Mittanian Kikkuli. He made a study of feeding and systematic exercise for his chariot horses. With an estimated 3500 chariots each pulled by three or four horses, he must have had a lot of experience!

But it was not until about 400 BC that the next known writings were published, by the great nobleman Xenophon. He made a great study of the horse, his needs, temperament and wellbeing. He decreed a cobby well-muscled type of horse most suitable for riding – which was hardly surprising since they rode bareback: saddles and stirrups had not then been invented! Even in those days the more quality or high-spirited horse demanded a much higher price than did a more placid animal. His explanations of how to handle and ride a horse are as practical today as in those days. For instance, he is quoted as declaring 'Never tend to a horse when you are in a passion', and 'What a horse does under compulsion is done without understanding, and there is no beauty in it either, any more than if one should whip or spur a dancer. There would be a great deal more ungracefulness than beauty in either horse or man that was so treated. No, he should show off all his finest and most brilliant performances willingly and at a mere sign.' These statements are written by a real horseman, and his teachings have helped riders and trainers for millenia to train their horses in a thoughtful and humane way, in spite of the fact that the horse during most of that time was generally used for battle. Even so, Xenophon had a definitely quiet approach to his training and expected his horses to be obedient and responsive to the lightest of aids.

THE RENAISSANCE HORSE

It was not until the Renaissance that the importance of dressage really grew, when princes and noblemen travelled to the great schools of Europe to study the art of horsemanship. The first riding school was set up in Naples in 1532 by Federico Grisone, where horsemasters experimented with different methods of training horses. They performed intricate movements and, from this, evolved the earliest form of dressage. Unfortunately, many of the horses went through considerable discomfort, through the ignorance of their trainers or simple lack of physical muscular ability.

In the late sixteenth century, another riding school started in Versailles, catering for the fashionable nobility of the day, but this disappeared during the Revolution. For a time nothing took its place until, in 1735, the Imperial Spanish Riding School opened in Vienna.

The early Egyptians Horses were domesticated from as early as 1650 BC by the Egyptians, both for work in the fields and for general transport. Note that the horses shown in this illustration are not yet being ridden.

THE IMPERIAL SPANISH RIDING SCHOOL OF VIENNA

For over 400 years the classical art of dressage has been practised at the Spanish Riding School, and it is on this that we base our training. Over the years, the masters have learned and developed sound basic principles for the training and muscular strengthening of a horse so that, within three or four years, he is able to accept the necessary collection and impulsion for such difficult movements as pirouette, piaffe and passage.

In Vienna, horse and rider are also taught the 'Airs Above the Ground' or *Haute Ecole*. These are refined techniques, but based on movements which are natural to the horse, and which one can often see horses performing when turned loose in the field. *Haute Ecole* movements are not used in classical competition dressage, but are unique to the Spanish Riding School. In the Levade, the horse balances with all his weight on the hindquarters, the hind

Lipizzaner horses of the Spanish Riding School in Vienna. This equestrian establishment is the greatest of all riding schools where the classical movements are still taught and performed. Some of these movements were originally used to outwit enemies in battle, and were practised and documented by the Italian and French riding masters of the sixteenth and seventeenth centuries. At the Spanish Riding School today, great emphasis is still placed on the correct seat and the position of the rider, as well as the thorough training and discipline of the horse. Regular displays of the classical movements are given to the public in the magnificent hall of the school in Vienna. Riders and horses also travel extensively abroad to give displays.

(Above) **John Lassiter's team** uses Lipizzaner horses to demonstrate the art of classical dressage in Great Britain.

(Above) Riders and horses from the **Cadre Noir** – an equestrian establishment that evolved from the French Military Riding School.

legs well bent under the belly, and the forelegs bent close to the chest. The body is at an angle of about 45° to the ground, and the horse stays motionless for a few seconds in this position. From this movement, the horse may have the agility to go forward into the Corbette. For this, he assumes the Levade position and then makes several jumps without his forelegs touching the ground. The most advanced movement of all is the Capriole, when the horse leaps into the air with his body horizontal and, when at full height, kicks out violently with both hind legs. For the knights of the past this movement was a useful way of repelling enemy pursuers. Of course, to obtain mastery of horsemanship at this level requires much study and training.

In its early years, the Spanish Riding School became the school to which all the kings and princes of Europe came to acquire the riding skills that were considered an essential attribute of their position. The main aims of the Spanish Riding School today are:

■ To safeguard for future generations the original principles of the equestrian art.

■ To demonstrate them to the public in displays of riding given twice a week in Vienna.

■ To uphold the highest standards and the classical principles in the art of dressage by producing trainers.

These principles are the accepted doctrine of the FEI (Fédération Equestre Internationale), which is the body that controls dressage competitions worldwide. The Spanish Riding School also controls the breeding of the Lipizzaner horse by testing the stallions and only allowing the best, who have proved their ability in this unique classical school of equitation, to be used as sires.

THE FRENCH CAVALRY SCHOOL

Some 30 years after the founding of the Spanish Riding School, a French Cavalry School was set up in Saumur in 1768. Its select group of officers were known as the Cadre Noir, named after their uniforms of black with gold stripes and insignia. They were renowned for their dashing riding both across country and in the art of dressage. Using mostly Anglo-Norman horses, they have made a great contribution to dressage over the last two centuries with such masters as Pluvinel and de la Guerinière. The French approach is unique and employs much lighter and more humane techniques than those of Grisone's Italian school.

(Left) **Dutch Courage** undergoes last-minute preparations, before entering the arena at Goodwood. Boots or bandages are removed, and he is given a light sponge down, with a squirt of extra fly spray if necessary.

HORSEMEN WHO MADE HISTORY

There were two notable Englishmen who took up the art of dressage, much to the amazement of their contemporaries. They were William Cavendish, the First Duke of Newcastle, and James Fillis. The Duke of Newcastle was a great supporter of Charles I. When the King was deposed, the Duke of Newcastle fled to Holland where he set up his own school. Already an accomplished horseman, he learned still more from his continental friends and wrote several excellent books. His understanding and obvious love of his horses made him a master. When he later returned to England, he continued schooling and training horses. His second book, published in 1667, was entitled *A New Method to Dress Horses* and was, perhaps, the first reference to dressage in Britain. Unfortunately, his teachings were soon forgotten when foxhunting became the fashion in the seventeenth century.

The second notable Englishman, James Fillis, was born in 1834. Another true horseman, he went to France when young and studied with Baucher before setting up his own school in Paris. Some of his movements were more flamboyant than classical in technique, and indeed most

of his performances took place in the circus because there were no other places for display. However, as a horseman he was renowned, and he ended his riding days teaching at the Russian Cavalry School in Leningrad. He was respected everywhere for the way his horses performed with great suppleness, impulsion and straightness, and contemporary Russian technique is still based on the teachings of Fillis. His book *Breaking and Riding* is used extensively by enthusiasts even today.

TRAINING TODAY

Nowadays, trainers from Germany, Denmark and the Spanish Riding School have taught all over the world, and this has, naturally, stimulated up-and-coming riders and improved standards everywhere. It is with the same desire to try to help others to understand the horse and to get pleasure from riding and training him that I have put on paper some of my own experiences with horses. Most of all, I hope that I have been able in this book to convey the bond between man and horse which is what makes dressage such a wonderful art and sport.

CHAPTER TWO

THE DRESSAGE HORSE

CHOOSING A SUITABLE HORSE

POPULAR BREEDS

THE RIGHT TEMPERAMENT

TRAINING THE FOAL

Catherston Guardarosa, seen here as a two-month-old foal, receiving his first introduction to the discipline of being tied up. This lesson need only last for a few minutes: complete dressage training will take four more years' sustained work. However, the training and handling of the foal from the very first day of his life can make or mar the vital partnership between a dressage horse and rider.

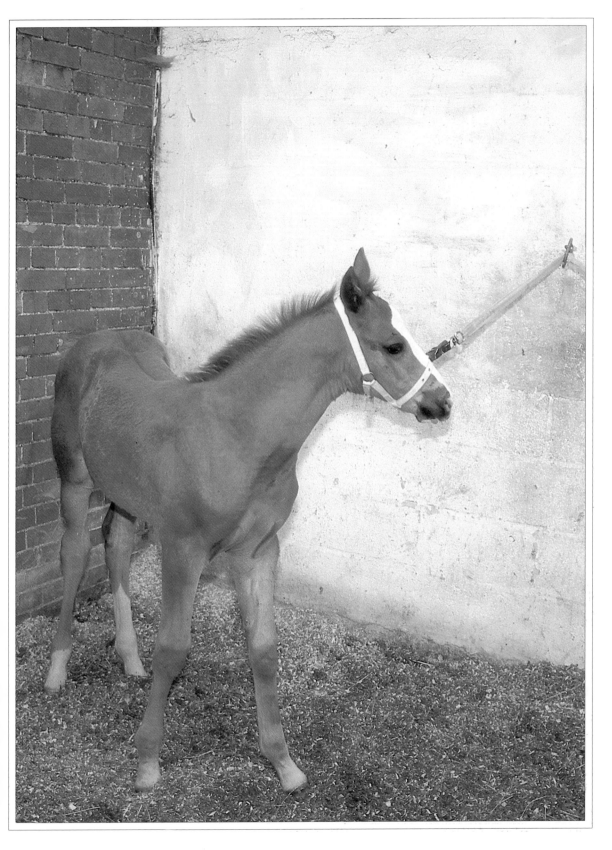

CHOOSING A SUITABLE HORSE

A dressage horse is trained only through the dedicated work and attention of his rider, but there are a number of pointers to consider when choosing a horse that might be suitable. It is important to choose a riding breed – neither a draught horse nor one so finely proportioned that he might not have enough strength to perform the prescribed dressage movements.

CONFORMATION

The ideal horse has a noble head and outlook, with the neck set not too low on the shoulders and the head clean, fine and flexible. He should have a well-laid shoulder with the elbow free. The chest should be deep but not too wide. The back should be strong and not hollow, with plenty of muscle over the loins. The croup should be long and not too flat. The foreleg should be strong with a well-muscled forearm. The knee should be well set and not slope backwards, and nor should the pastern and hoof angle which is under considerable strain. The hind leg should not be too straight but be well angled from the stifle – hock – hoof. The gaskin should be well muscled.

Correctly proportioned quality yearling. Note the fine but strong limbs, good outline and noble carriage. He has a good shoulder and very elegant head and neck. At the moment, he is distinctly higher behind than in front, but this will level out as he grows.

Three-quarter Thoroughbred – this horse has a good shoulder and length of neck. His head is well set on to his neck, and his strong back and overall compactness means he will find collected movements easy. He has enough bone for his size and weight. The fact that he is short from knee to fetlock means he is less likely to suffer strains to the tendons.

The correct outline. This horse has a very deep girth which gives him a lot of weight in front to control, but he has a lovely head, which is beautifully set on to his neck, as the neck is to the shoulder. The shoulder is sloping, so he will have plenty of freedom with his forelegs. He naturally stands with his hind legs well under him. Note his strongly muscled quarters.

PACES

The most important points to look for in a dressage horse are good paces and temperament. Correct conformation is important, for a well-made horse is naturally better balanced. The swing and elasticity of the paces are often born into a good horse but, with correct training, all horses can be greatly improved. Nevertheless, a horse who moves well commands a price at least double that of an average mover. The paces to look for when seeing a horse in hand or on the lunge are a free, swinging walk with the hind leg overtracking the front hoof prints by at least 152mm (six inches). The trot should be energetic with swing and elasticity in the steps, and there should be a clear moment of suspension between each step. The horse should be free in the shoulders, and his hocks should be active and show plenty of flexion. In canter, he should have a clear, three-beat step showing balance and swing off the ground. The stride should be of medium length and land lightly.

Showing his paces. Even at this early stage in a horse's life, you can judge the quality of paces and movement. Here the foal shows freedom of his shoulder and hind legs as he moves. His hocks are well bent beneath him, and his forelegs are easily stretched out. His steps are springy, as can be seen by the clear moment of suspension. The pace shows good swing and elasticity.

POPULAR BREEDS

There are many different types and breeds used for dressage, the most famous being the Lipizzaner, which is used at the Spanish Riding School in Vienna. They are mostly bred at Piber in Austria and in Yugoslavia, and descend from the Arab Barb and Andalusian horses. They are rather small, standing about 15.2hh, but are hardy, tough, long-lived and have a powerful, lively action. The tendency nowadays is to breed horses much bigger, so we may see more Lipizzaners in future competitions.

Modern dressage riders tend to use the Warmblood horse or cross-bred horse. There are quite a few areas in which cross-breeding has been established over many years. Germany has made a detailed study of pedigrees and there are performance tests for mares and stallions. The result of stock from all stallions is on computer so it is easy to discover the sires who are producing the most

winners in any discipline. The Holstein, Hanoverian and Westphalian are breeds from which some of the most successful horses have been cross-bred.

The Hanoverian is a big, free-moving, athletic horse and comes from crossing Carriage horses with Trakehner and Thoroughbred blood to make it the modern riding type we know today. The Holstein is another successful breed whose ancestry includes the Yorkshire Coach horse and Cleveland Bay refined with Thoroughbred blood. Westphalian horses are a mixture of Hanoverian, Oldenburg, Trakehner and Thoroughbred, and are another example of successful competition horses.

The Danish and Dutch horses are also very successful in dressage competitions. The Danish horse derives from famous lines from Germany, Sweden and the Thoroughbred. Holland has used similar methods,

Dutch Warmblood The offspring of a Groningen/ Gelderland cross mare and a Thoroughbred sire, this horse has strong limbs and a good shoulder. He has a noble head, clean gullet and deep barrel. His neck is well set on to his shoulder. Although he stands over a good amount of ground, he is well balanced.

Danish Warmblood This horse has Hanoverian, Swedish and Trakhener blood in his breeding. He is short-backed and strong, with his hind legs well under him. He is a little overweighted in front, and his neck is rather low set.

Hanoverian This horse has a neck very well set on to his shoulder, together with a clean gullet and a noble head. He has quite a good shoulder, but not a very pronounced wither. He has strong hind legs, and appears nicely balanced.

Trakehner A beautiful, extremely well balanced horse, showing the elegance of this breed. This stallion provides a perfect example of why the Trakehner has been used to lighten many of the warmblood breeds of Europe.

crossing their native Gelderland and Groningen mares with Thoroughbred, Holstein, Anglo-Norman and Trakehner stallions.

The Trakehner is one of the oldest breeds in Germany. It is one of the finest riding horses and comes from the Schweiken — a small, hardy, active draught horse — crossed with Thoroughbred and Arab blood. The Trakehner is used as a pure bred in dressage, eventing and show jumping, and has been crossed with nearly every Warmblood breed in Europe to help refine the native stock.

The Irish horse, descended from the Irish draught and the Thoroughbred, has produced many top competition horses — mostly show jumpers, but there have been some successful dressage horses too. The British Warmblood Society founded in 1977 has had great success in a short time, using mostly graded stallions from Germany, Holland and Denmark and crossing them with English graded mares, mostly Thoroughbred. Dutch Gold and Catherston Dutch Bid, both registered as British Warmbloods, are international dressage horses and are used to illustrate this book.

BREEDING THE DRESSAGE HORSE

TEMPERAMENT (See also Chapter 3, p.30)

When breeding for dressage, it is important not only to look at the conformation and action of the sire and dam, but also to find out how co-operative they both were as riding horses themselves. Did they have open, generous natures? Was either temperamental or nappy? Did they enjoy working for the rider? Did either have difficult habits?

You can learn a lot from the outlook of a horse and how he behaves when handled. (Of course, bad handling or teasing can make any horse sour and bad tempered.) The head and ears tell you most about a horse. A large, kind eye and a broad, flat forehead with neat ears set well apart are important pointers when buying or breeding a dressage horse. A naturally inquisitive foal usually develops into a generous, bold riding horse. Dressage does require a lot of sustained effort from a horse so the

Warmblood foal A good illustration of a well-made, strong filly foal, bred from a Hanoverian stallion and a Hanoverian-cross-Thoroughbred mare. Her hind legs are strong; the forelegs slightly bent over at the knee, but this is a good fault. She has a good head, well set on to the neck, and a good shoulder. Note how she carries her head in an attractive and natural arch. Altogether, she displays a lot of bone and will be a big, strong, quality mare when fully grown.

right keen temperament is required. After all, there is no point spending years in training only to find a horse is sluggish or lacking in spirit and never gives you his best. On the other hand, a horse who is very nervous and easily overexcited can really let you down on a big occasion when the atmosphere is electric. The very timid, spooky horse is not an easy ride in the arena and can cause many nervous crises for his rider too! Personally, I love a threequarter Thoroughbred horse with the other quarter being Warmblood or Irish.

A PERFECT PARTNER

As a rider you must, of course, think what sort of horse is going to suit your character. If you are tall and have a highly-strung nature, you will need a big horse with a quiet temperament which you can fire with enthusiasm. However, someone without great reserves of physical strength should look for a much smaller and more sensitive horse with plenty of energy. The compatibility of horse and rider is of vital importance because dressage really is the bonding together of a great partnership and, if you do not suit each other temperamentally and physically, then you should not even attempt to begin training. The rider's personality makes a major contribution to the performance – a good rider can enhance a horse's natural presence and turn him into a star performer.

The various kinds of temperament are explored in more detail in Chapter 3, showing how you can make the most of your horse in your approach to his training.

TRAINING THE FOAL

If you are breeding your own dressage horse and have selected an appropriate stallion, checked the premises and made sure that the stud is suitable, then all you have to do is wait eleven months for the happy event. Of course, in the meantime you must keep a careful eye on the mare, feeding her according to the weather and her condition. And when she finally foals, you will, marvel that he is going to be your dressage horse in four years' time.

A successful delivery, and the mare nuzzles and licks her **newborn foal.** Within an hour or two, the foal should begin struggling to his feet, and he will soon take his first drink. Even this early in a horse's life, some idea of temperament and character can be gained by observing the foal's movements – whether they are bold and daring, or cautious and nervous.

The rider can learn an immense amount about his horse from the moment of his birth and it is an event I never miss. As the foal strives to stand up in the first few hours of life, you will see the first evidence of his character. Is he keen and alert, or weak and easily put off? How determined is he to find his mother's milk? Is your presence noticed, and is he fearful or inquisitive? When he is turned out, how does he carry himself? Has he that innate presence and carriage which make a natural star, or are you hoping to turn him into one?

After the first six to eight weeks, provided he has been well done by his dam, he will have filled out and be score over men because women are naturally more gentle. When you first touch a foal, it should be with the looking his best. On the whole he will be more or less the same shape at six years as he is at six weeks, so study him then and imagine him fully mature. This is the first opportunity you have to predict the future.

EARLY HANDLING

A foal's early training should start on Day One of his life. The most important part of riding and training horses is to have 'feel' in your hands. This is where women tend to back of the fingers in a soft stroking motion up the crest of the neck or along the top of the back. Your finges must be made to feel as much like a mare's muzzle as possible — then the foal will feel you are part of the family.

It is natural for all animals to be disciplined and, in this case, it usually starts with the mare giving her foal a nip when he is too rough or boisterous. Your first lesson with the foal should start with a stable rubber slipped round his neck and a hand behind his quarters. The rubber is the restraint and your hand the impulsion and great care must be taken at this stage to prevent him getting frightened and hurting himself. Gradually, as he has a foal slip placed on his head and is taught to lead, he will learn to respect you as his master.

The more you can get a foal used to being handled in the first week of his life, the better. Feeling his legs, looking into his mouth, picking up his feet, and so on are ways of making him familiar with what he will encounter in later life. If he is led in and out of the field daily, that will be all that is necessary at this age. When he is six to eight weeks old, the blacksmith should be asked to trim his feet and he should have his first worm dose. Within a few weeks of birth he should be leading well alongside his mother. He should be easy to catch and have a healthy respect for you without being fearful.

Discipline is vital and the trainer-handler must be aware of any potential problems which could become dangers in later life. Nipping, for instance, could become biting. Standing on his hind legs and kicking are both natural habits to a foal, but he must realize that you do not approve. If you have to reprimand him for some misdemeanour then use your eyes, voice, and make a sharp movement of your arms and, if necessary, a smack with the hand. The eyes of the trainer are very important. The mare reprimands her offspring by laying back her ears (showing anger), fixing her gaze on the foal (attack) and giving him a sharp nip or a tap with the hind leg (pain as punishment). She will also praise her offspring by a lick, nuzzle him with the end of her nose or give him a soft adoring look. The trainer must take up this role of parennntal discipline and incorporate it as an essential element in training. A horse is extremely fast in his reactions, and the trainer must reflect this, instantaneously administering any form of praise or punishment. The voice should be used as an aid — a growl used in conjunction with a stern and angry look is a warning. Kind, soothing words, a soft, affectionate look and a gentle touch on the neck denote pleasure and appreciation.

A disciplined horse is a happy one. He has security in knowing your mood. He will respect your authority just

The pretty, well proportioned **head of a promising youngster.** His pricked ears show his alertness and awareness of his surroundings; he is showing the whites of his eyes simply because he is taking an interest in what is going on to his left!

as, if running with a herd, he would have his pecking order. You are the boss and he will be happy to submit to this and know you will guide and protect him.

When the foal is leading well beside his dam and he responds to a light pull on the lead rope, you can dispense with the hand behind his quarters. He has learned all he needs of discipline for the moment, and his well-being should be your only consideration. He must be allowed to enjoy his early childhood, playing in the field, his dam caring for him and teaching him.

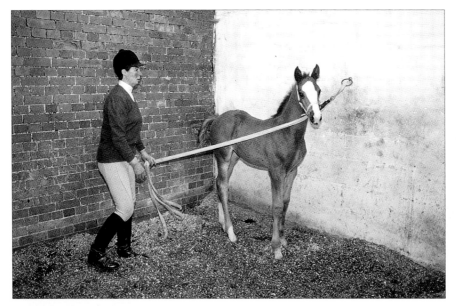

Handling the foal.
These pictures illustrate a two-month-old foal's first introduction to being tied up. The lessons are taking place in the stable with a deep layer of shavings on the floor. This provides a safe grounding; he will not slip on the shavings as he might on straw, and the depth of the shavings offers protection should he fall.
I To begin with, the handler should stand behind the foal, so that if he pulls back, the rein can be flipped behind him to encourage him forward.

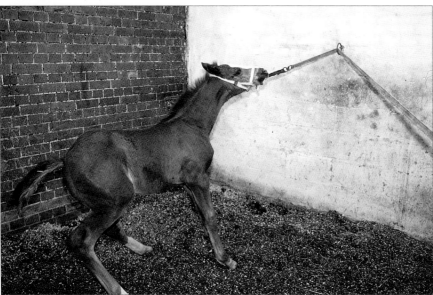

2 After this, the handler should move away, so that the foal learns that he must be on his own.

TYING UP THE FOAL

At about six months of age and a few weeks after weaning, the foal must learn to be tied up. It is usually better to teach this discipline to a young horse when he has been playing in the field and is then settled in the stable. There should be plenty of bedding on the floor to prevent slipping. If the foal is very big and strong then a thick neck strap should be put round the top of his neck and attached to the rope by a ring. Thread the rope through the noseband and throat strap of the head collar to keep the pressure coming down the head so that the foal cannot

throttle himself. Usually, the foal will tie up happily while you are with him in the stable but he must also learn to be left alone while tied up. Gradually, if left for ten minutes a day, your foal will come to accept that he cannot get away. Of course, you should always be near by until he is accustomed to the idea. Then, gradually, he should be tied up for at least an hour occasionally to make sure he does not fight the rope.

I can never see any point in the practice of tying up a horse to a string that breaks if he pulls back. This just teaches the horse to fight the rope, and he becomes a menace and a danger to himself and everyone dealing

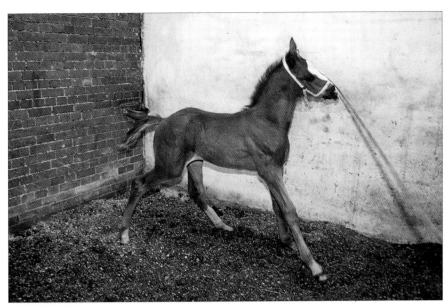

3 The foal has to be both independent and disciplined.

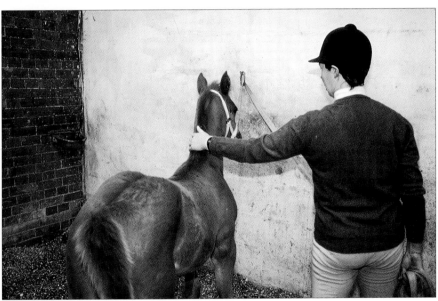

4 When the foal moves forward and stands quietly, he should be rewarded with a loose lead-line, and a stroke on the neck. He will then understand that this bit of discipline – which should last for only a few minutes – is appreciated by the handler.

with him. It is difficult to get a fully-grown horse out of the habit of pulling back. However, if the foal is taught properly the problem will never occur.

Finally, always take great care where you tie up a horse. Check to ensure you have not chosen an insecure ring or a railing which may come adrift.

Your young foal now needs only daily care of feeding, grooming and exercise. If he is kept in the field then there is little handling required, so leave him alone, except for assuring yourself of his condition and well-being. Young horses who are too much fussed over can easily lose their respect, so just let him grow on and enjoy himself.

Some people like to show their horses as youngsters. This is often a good thing in moderation because the young horse learns to travel. At the same time, he gets used to the sights and sounds of a show and so is less excited when he is older than one who has never left home. If you do show a youngster, it is important that he is not pulled about with a bit in his mouth. Make sure he does not have his natural paces ruined by poor leading, nor have his freedom of movement cramped.

When the horse has reached the autumn of his third year, then is the time for his education as a riding horse to begin.

CHAPTER THREE

MAKING THE MOST OF YOUR HORSE

UNDERSTANDING HIS TEMPERAMENT

LUNGING

INTRODUCING THE RIDER

THE CORRECT SEAT

THE RIDING AIDS

Catherston Romeo, seen here fully equipped for lunging. He is at the stage of training where, now he is used to wearing a saddle, bridle and side reins, he is ready to be ridden on the lunge. The early work on the lunge is an important first step on the road to training a dressage horse.

UNDERSTANDING HIS TEMPERAMENT

All horses have different temperaments, and as a rider you must try to understand the way your particular horse thinks. In Chapter 2 (see p.20) we have already considered the importance of the dressage horse's sire and dam, and the role played by the temperament of his rider, in determining his character. But you can also ask yourself the following questions in order to form an accurate judgment of your horse.

Is he bold and brave? Is he timid and nervous? Is he lazy and lacking energy? Is he looking for trouble or lacking confidence? Is he highly charged and running away with himself?

You will have noticed his characteristics when you first started training your horse on the lunge, but some will not manifest themselves until you start to ride him out in the woods and fields by himself. If we consider each type of temperament in turn, it may help you to progress to a better understanding of your horse.

BOLD AND BRAVE

This is the type of horse I like. You can spot horses with this temperament at an early age in the field — as foals, they walk up and sniff anything unusual, and acquire a sense of confidence on their own. These horses are usually free and forward-going to ride, and only need the occasional bit of reassurance given to them, such as a stroke on the neck when something fearful appears. They are quick-thinking, so can also be keen to try to get their own way; the rider must be aware of this and not allow any behaviour that might grow into a bad habit. These horses are usually quite sensitive, so if and when any reprimand is needed, it should not be too sharp, and praise must be quickly given when appropriate.

TIMID AND NERVOUS

This type of horse requires a rider with the ability to be relaxed and placid. With correct handling, these horses can become excellent riding horses, but they must be given time and patience. They are often very spooky and jumpy to ride when young, so the rider must have a firm and independent seat. If the horse jumps at some object, the rider makes things worse if he loses his balance. Losing his balance, the rider will probably have jerked the horse in the mouth and roughly kicked him as well, and

(Above) In this picture of **Wily Trout**, his trot steps are good, but his ears show him to be a little nervous. In fact this horse, once much misunderstood, has been carefully retrained and transformed into a world-class dressage horse by Christopher Bartle.

(Above) Here **Marzog** shows complete harmony and understanding with his rider. Note how his ears and eyes show interest and relaxation, and there is no tension in his appearance and movement. He has always appeared to have an ideal temperament — generous and willing.

A world-class dressage horse – **Marco Polo** – performing a left half-pass, and caught in an unfortunate moment! The horse is showing tension and is overbent in the head and neck. He has stepped sideways very easily but has lost his self-carriage, which the rider is trying to regain.

the horse will then view whatever he jumped at as a source of pain too. With a young horse, this could cause it to rear up on its hind legs from the association of pain, and to bolt or buck from his sense of fear, so there could be a nasty accident. But the same horse, correctly handled and ridden, will settle. If a nervous horse spooks or jumps at some object, time must be taken with him so that the horse gains confidence. Show him the object carefully, making sure you use a firm but allowing hand, and with your legs closed round the horse's body. Stroke him on the neck to reassure him, and if he is being constantly stupid every day at the same place, then ride him firmly forward, allowing him to keep his own distance from the object, and by degrees give him plenty to do until he stops finding that object dangerous. The better educated the horse becomes, the easier it is to overcome his nervousness. As he answers the leg and seat aids correctly, then you can place him in shoulder-in away from the objects he is likely to spook at, and thus overcome his nerves. Sometimes these timid horses can use spooking as an evasion of work, and it is important for the rider to have the experience to recognize this fact and to overcome it with fair, firm treatment of the young

horse. It always saddens me to see an inexperienced rider hit a young horse with the whip because he spooked. The mind of a spooky horse is usually so concentrated on the object of fear that any pain inflicted on him at this time makes things worse because he then thinks the object itself hit him. There is a fine balance to be maintained with these horses in understanding the way in which their minds work, and dealing with them. You must have patience and firmness with the young horse, but you must rely on your legs and seat, then you can build up that confidence between the rider and horse which is so important in a good combination.

LAZY AND LACKING IN ENERGY

This temperament is often associated with big, young horses or rather common, heavy horses. I have found that some three-year-olds can appear thick-skinned, so that a sharp flick with the whip has no effect: they do not register or associate the pain from the whip as a stimulus because the nervous system is not fully developed. You will be able to identify these horses when you first come to lunge them, and they are best left for another six to nine

An Olympic and World Champion horse – **Granat** – whose temperament was far from easy. With careful dedicated training from Georg Wahl and his rider Christine Stuckelberger, he became a star in the arena. Here he is showing interest and obedience to his rider, listening to the aid he is being given to turn right. The rider is in the correct position, resulting in her horse being beautifully balanced.

months before trying to ride them. However, I must point out that I have only had two such horses in 40 years and one of these was an immature pony! So this condition is a rare one. The lazy horse, on the other hand, is often encountered, and his training must be short and sharp. The diet should be made up of energy foods and all hay should be removed for two to three hours before you are going to work the horse. Make sure your forward aids are not muddled by the rein aids, and give a lot of praise and even a titbit when he is responsive. These horses need plenty of variety in their work. Try not to get them tired, but increase their work by degrees as they become fitter.

LOOKING FOR TROUBLE, OR LACKING CONFIDENCE

These problems usually occur with the older horse, although lack of confidence may also characterize some very young animals. In addition, any of the previously mentioned types of horse can use this trait as an evasion. Horses may become nappy and disobedient for many reasons. Unfortunately it is usually the rider who is at fault. Perhaps he has not felt the horse holding back his forward movement, and corrected this with just one little reminder with the whip. Or he may have demanded too

In this picture, **Dutch Courage** is showing complete confidence and harmony in the movement he is performing. His ears show his interest, but he is listening attentively to his rider. His steps are free and flowing, although his forehand could be a little lighter. When young, this horse was extremely volatile and as a result, occasional moments of disobedience were experienced! However, his generosity and willingness have made him a wonderful competition horse – one who would always rise to a big occasion.

much of the horse too soon, making the horse rebel in mind and body against the rider. The horse may have been abused by bad riding, or become bored by too much repetition. Or there may be some physical disorder which is giving the horse pain, such as sharp teeth, azoturia or back pain. Having investigated and checked against all the above possibilities, you then have the problem of correcting the evasion. Often I find the horse is bored and has not been given enough to occupy his mind. Transitions, turns, circles of different sizes, and so on can be used as ways of overcoming this. Trotting poles and small jumps is another good method of giving your horse something different to think about. Providing a change of scene through hacking out, or giving him a gallop with another horse can be enjoyable and beneficial for both horse and rider. The motto, 'All work and no play makes Jack a dull boy,' is true for both you and the horse. Do not get bogged down with dressage!

HIGHLY CHARGED AND RUNNING AWAY WITH HIMSELF

This temperament is quite common with highly bred Thoroughbred types. Some horses have little natural rhythm to their paces and are rather highly strung and over-sensitive. With such horses, the rider must be positive and calm. He must be sure to have his legs firmly but encouragingly round the horse, and his restraining aids may have to be overused for a time, until the horse learns to listen to the repeated use of the half-halt. These horses must be made to wait and to listen to the forward-driving aids. Because they are very sensitive, they tend to try to run away from everything. So you must teach them from the very beginning that there is nothing to fear from the legs, they must just accept them and slow down. It takes a little time and patience to get these horses to settle; often they need only to be asked to walk for sufficiently long to achieve balance in the walk. If they are too nervous to walk, then trot very slowly on a large circle until the horse gradually settles and mentally unwinds. Think solely of establishing rhythm and a slow, slow pace; then, when the horse thinks he would like to stop, that is the time to ride him forward with your seat and legs, until he accepts these aids. After a few weeks of long, slow work the horse will accept your legs and seat, and gain a rhythm, but you must keep him under control and never allow him to run on. The same will apply when riding him out, and extreme patience is required. Only when the horse is really prepared to listen to you in walk and trot should you begin work on the canter.

Having considered the most common kinds of temperament found in horses and the earliest stages of handling, we can turn to the process of training them in earnest. Always bear in mind that a horse only performs according to the ability of the rider, so it is to oneself one must look when things go wrong.

LUNGING THE HORSE

This is one of the most important aspects of training the young horse, and it is a practice which can be used at any time during a horse's training.

Equipment needed is a snaffle bridle, cavesson, lunge rein, lunge whip, roller and/or saddle, side reins, and boots on all four legs. The handler needs sensible, strong, flat boots and gloves.

LUNGING — THE PRELIMINARIES

When starting a young horse on the lunge, I always like to check his teeth to make sure he has no sharp points on the molars which could hurt when the cavesson is firmly adjusted round the nose. 'Wolf teeth', if your horse has them, are generally better removed before you ever try to put a bit in his mouth. Wolf teeth are tiny teeth found just in front of the molars, and usually only on the upper jaw. Some vets try to persuade you not to bother with their removal, but in my experience they upset all horses and, once a biting habit is formed in a horse's mind, he never forgets. Some horses can be so uncomfortable with a bit in their mouth when they have wolf teeth that they become rather violent, throw their heads all over the place and hate to close their mouths round the bit because these tiny teeth touch it and give them pain. Your vet can remove the teeth quite simply and, after a week to allow healing, you can start to lunge your horse.

I find the best age to start lunging and breaking in your horse is the autumn of his third year. More unruly horses could be started as late two-year-olds or early three-year-olds, but care must be taken only to lunge them on large circles and for short periods. The bigger the horse, the longer he needs to mature and develop. Remember, it is the joints which suffer later if a horse is overworked too young.

When starting to lunge a horse, an area of flat ground approximately 20 metres (22 yards) across and situated somewhere quiet is desirable. It is also an advantage to the handler if the area is enclosed in some way, with a temporary fence of rails or hurdles. An indoor arena is, of course, ideal

THE BENEFITS OF LUNGING

Lunging is one of the first opportunities the trainer has to form a relationship with his horse. It teaches the horse to obey the commands of 'Walk on', 'Trot', 'Whoa', and later,

'Canter'. It muscles the horse up, so that his back becomes stronger and more able to accept the weight of the rider. It helps him to balance and to become more supple. If your horse is taught to lunge correctly, he can be beautifully balanced and able to accept the bit before he is ever ridden. Then, once he has adjusted to the rider's weight, within days he will become a lovely riding horse, capable of understanding the aids of the rider very quickly.

When starting horses on the lunge I use only a cavesson, lunge rein, boots on all four legs and a lunge whip. First lead the horse around the area he is to be lunged in, so that he is familiar with his surroundings. Talk to him, saying, 'Walk on', and if he is hanging behind, touch him with the lunge whip, which is in your left hand. As soon as he walks up level with your shoulder say 'Good boy' in a soothing voice, and stroke him on the neck. Then teach him to 'Whoa', giving little jerks on the lunge rein and using your voice at the same time. As soon as any response is seen, reward him with 'Good boy' and a stroke on the neck. If this is repeated many times, the horse will soon listen to you and know 'Walk on' and 'Whoa'.

STARTING THE HORSE ON THE LUNGE

Now is the time to start lunging him properly. I find many people get into trouble at this point because they do not understand the way a horse's mind works. He has learnt that you have a long arm which can bite, ie the stick, and that you can also prevent him from running away with the cavesson and rein. The one is apt to bite, and the other is a check, and it is very important not to confuse the two in the early stages. The horse must first go forward as you say, 'Walk on', and you may also have to touch him or even flick him with the whip to encourage him forward and away from you. Here it is important to let him move away from you, so do not contradict the command by giving a jerk on the cavesson just as the horse has obeyed the forward command. You must allow him to go forward with the rein, even if he goes straight away on the left rein in trot. This does not matter. Encourage him to go forward in a walk if possible, or in trot if not, and guide him as to where he is to go with the lunge rein and by means of your stance. The whip is an indication to go forward, and shifting slightly in the direction the horse is to go will help you move him away from you. Never step away from the horse to shorten the lunge rein, or this will encourage him to decrease the size of the circle and to come at you. If the

horse is cutting the size of the circle, look him fiercely in the eye and step attackingly towards him with the stick pointed at his shoulder. As he responds, soften your look and return the whip to the correct position.

ACHIEVING THE CORRECT CONTACT

Having achieved forward movement on the circle, only then teach the horse the correct tension on the lunge rein. Do not allow him to be too strong and to lean away from you by pulling hard on the lunge rein. If he leans on it, indicate once again the tension which is comfortable to you both, and which should only be a light contact, by lightening your hand whenever you can, and talking in a soothing way when he is correct. If he is very strong, then you must give little jerks on the rein until he comes lighter on the contact. Of course, you will not teach the horse to have the correct contact on the first day, but sometimes one is lucky. All horses should be lunged on both reins, but if you have a horse who has taken time to understand how to lunge on day one, then that is not the day to start lunging on the right rein too, as this would overwork him. The right rein can be taught the next day. Always finish the lesson when real obedience comes, because the last things a horse learns are the ones he will get up with the next day.

Lunging: The correct equipment
(Top) The horse is wearing a cavesson, a snaffle bridle with side reins attached, a saddle, breastplate, and boots on all four legs. The bridle is put on first, and the cavesson *(Close-up, above)* is slipped over the top. The noseband pieces fit under the cheekpieces of the bridle, so as not to interfere with the action of the bit. The cavesson must also be high enough not to pinch the horse's lips if the reins are used.

LUNGING ON THE RIGHT REIN

It is usually more difficult to lunge a horse on the right rein, because very few people ever bother to lead a horse from both sides. It is always considered correct to lead a horse from the near (left) side, but by doing this one is constantly asking him to bend slightly to the left, otherwise he is apt to step on you if he is allowed to look away from you and you are not fully in control of him. I like to get my young horses used to leading correctly from both sides early on in their foal years, so there is no problem later.

When you start to lunge the horse on the right rein, repeat the process you used on the left rein by walking with him on the circle to start with, and then asking him to lunge as soon as he is confident. In just a few days the horse should have learnt to lunge easily on both reins, and to obey 'Walk', 'Trot' and 'Whoa'.

If you have not reached this stage within four days then you must review your ability as a trainer, for you cannot have taught your horse fairly if he remains confused and disobedient.

INTRODUCING THE BIT AND ROLLER

On the whole, by day three I like to introduce the horse to the bit. I prefer a lightweight, loose ring snaffle as a general rule, but if the horse is rather fussy then a cheek snaffle with keepers is a good bit to use, especially if the horse is apt to put his tongue over the bit. If you have a horse with a dry mouth, a little honey put on the bit will sometimes

help. The bit must be correctly fitted, bearing in mind the different actions of the various types of bit.

A day or so later, the horse can be introduced to the roller. It is important always to have a breastplate on a young horse so that you can start with the girth very loose. A webbing girth, or one with elastic to start with, will have some give in it, should the horse really puff himself out against the girth. The less fuss at this stage the more confidence the horse will have in all you do with him, so common-sense handling in the early days is paramount.

THE SIDE REINS

When the horse is happy to have the roller put on and the girth adjusted quite firmly, you can start to introduce him to the side reins. There are several types of side rein: plain leather, leather with rubber or elastic insert, etc. I find the ones with elastic more like your hand, and the rein is of course less severe. With horses who are apt to lean on the rein, it is better to use the all-leather reins because these teach the horse to lighten the contact and give a quicker reaction to the contact.

When fitting the side reins you must start with them very loose, and shorten them gradually over several days. The side reins should be the same length, and it is important to check them every time you shorten them by standing in front of the horse and pulling the ends of the reins towards you. The purpose of lunging with side reins is to help the horse balance himself, to teach him to maintain a light contact with the reins, to control the circling force of the lunge, and to contain the horse's

Lunging a young horse
(Top left) Here the horse is pulling away from the trainer with his head bent in. Correct by applying gentle pressure on the outside side rein.

(Top right) A good demonstration of how a horse usually reacts in the same way at the same point on the circle. Here he is considering running out of the circle, but the trainer has anticipated this and has corrected it with a firm, but giving rein. The horse is responding by staying on the arc of the circle.
(Above) The horse is lunging correctly, responding to a light contact on the lunge rein. He is moving freely forward in a nicely balanced outline.

outside shoulder. When the horse is used to the side reins and carrying himself in the correct outline, with his neck nicely arched from the wither and the front of his face just in front of the vertical line, then you may progress to a saddle. With all lunging, it is important that the horse is driven forward into the side reins, not just shortened up until they are tight and then driven into them. This will upset the horse and could cause him to resist and rear up, or run backwards and put his tongue over the bit.

Once the horse is going forward in a relaxed manner seeking the bit, then you can shorten the reins by a couple of holes at a time, until you have the horse taking an even feel on the outside side rein. You will find that you are able to drive him quietly forward with the whip, containing the energy with the lunge rein which also indicates the bend and direction of the circle.

INTRODUCING THE SADDLE

When introducing the saddle to the horse, as with the roller, it is important to use a breastplate until you know he is happy to be girthed up sufficiently tightly to ensure the saddle is not going to slip. When the horse is confident of the different feel of the saddle, you can again put on the side reins and adjust them higher or lower, depending on the age and stage of training of the horse. Sometimes it is a good idea to fit the roller over the saddle and have several rings at different levels down each side, so that the side reins stay at the height you require. Alternatively, you can thread them through the two girth straps. When the horse is happy with the saddle, introduce the stirrups and fit them so that they hang between the end of the saddle flap and the horse's elbow. Let the horse get used to these moving about against his sides.

LONG-REINING

Now is the time you should start either to back him or to long-rein him. The latter is not easy and is not recommended for a beginner, but it is most helpful in the training of the young horse, and for later training too, because a horse has greater trust in you and is much easier to ride after you have done a little long-reining. Start by attaching the second lunge rein on to the outside ring of the cavesson and through the outside stirrup, which has been tied under the horse's belly to the other stirrup to stop it flying up. I prefer to have the rein run through the stirrup rather than the ring of a roller as it releases tension much quicker. I ask an assistant to hold the horse on the near side, while I walk at a safe distance on the off side with the second rein round behind the horse. Once at a safe distance, let the horse feel the rein by allowing it to touch him on the offside hind leg, just above the hock. Do this several times, until the horse appears happy and relaxed. Then, returning to his side, collect up the rein and put it on the top of the saddle. Go to the near side, place the offside rein across the top of the horse's croup, and with the end of that rein in your right hand, start to lunge him in the normal way, holding the near side rein in the left hand. When the horse is happily in walk, flick the right rein so that it drops over his quarters and swings round his hind legs. The horse may become a bit nervous at this point and rush off, but as long as you yourself do not panic or pull on the outside rein, he will soon find nothing hurts him and settle down.

As the horse becomes accustomed to the rein, you can begin to use it a little. Some small flicks with the rein will activate the hind legs, and a light constant pressure on the rein will decrease the speed, together with the use of your voice. When the horse is listening to your commands you can change the rein and repeat the procedure on the other rein, until the horse is relaxed and happy on both reins.

The horse can also be driven with both reins attached to the bit, but this does require someone with very light hands and a lot of experience. I have long-reined some young horses before backing them, and have found them extremely easy to ride afterwards. In this case, run both reins through the stirrups and drive the horse first on the circle at walk and trot, then back to walk and change the rein out of the circle. Continue with this until the horse is obedient and confident about the up and downward transitions and the changes of direction. Then you can drive the horse in walk round the school, encouraging him forward gently with the reins, and directing him with a very light hand. So often people are too strong with the directing reins and thereby destroy a good mouth. For this reason, I would suggest that only an experienced or very thoughtful person use this method.

RIDING ON THE LUNGE

At this stage, the horse is ready to ride on the lunge. This should be done by someone with a balanced seat, and not a beginner. Mounting is best done by giving the rider a 'leg up', because this does not shift the saddle and places the weight of the rider directly on the horse. Some people like to lean across the saddle to start with, before mounting properly. In my experience, the more often you get on and off the horse the more accustomed he becomes to strange things happening. When you first move off, just walk a few steps and stop. Reassure the horse and get off and on again if you think he looks nervous. If he is quiet, move on again, keeping a close watch on how he is reacting, and stopping before he ever gets upset. I always make my riders hold on to the pommel until the horse is used to the idea of someone on his back. The rider can then be sure he stays with the horse without losing his balance or letting his weight suddenly bang on the horse's back, should the horse start off, or buck, or make unusual movements. Some riders prefer a neck strap, but these can slip round if you do lose balance.

MOUNTING

Once the horse has become accustomed to the rider being given a leg up, then you must teach him to accept the rider mounting correctly from the ground.

Place the left foot in the left stirrup and swing the right

Mounting a young horse for the first time.

1 The trainer stands at the horse's head and reassures him with voice and hand throughout the exercise. An assistant gives the rider a leg-up, but initially the rider just balances across the saddle. All movements should be as quiet and smooth as possible.

2 The rider now balances across the saddle, while the trainer continues to reassure the horse about this strange occurrence. Providing he is calm and unflustered, the horse could be moved forward a few steps with the rider leaning across the saddle in this position.

3 The horse, having taken little notice of the rider across his back, and being confident about this new experience, is now mounted. With further assistance from the helper, the rider puts her right leg across the saddle, taking great care not to touch the horse's back with her leg. The trainer continues to reassure the horse.

4 The rider settles herself gently into the saddle, putting both feet in the stirrups and holding onto the pommel and neck strap. When the horse is confident and relaxed, the trainer, still reassuring him, moves him forward to take the first few steps with a rider on his back. He is then halted and reassured once again.

Riding on the lunge

1 Once the first few steps with a rider on the horse's back have been taken, the horse can be lunged with a rider. To begin with, the trainer stands at the horse's head, reassuring him so that he is completely confident about what is to take place.

2 The trainer has moved away from the horse's head and is starting to lunge him at a walk. All the initiative and instruction comes from the trainer; the rider is merely a passenger and should not attempt to give the horse any aids or commands.

3 The horse is happily accepting his rider and is going forward calmly on the lunge in working trot. Just how long it will take for a horse to accept a rider in this way depends very much on each individual animal. The trainer must judge how far he can progress in each session, according to how happily and confidently the horse is reacting.

Fitting the lunge rein

Ideally, a young horse should be lunged with a rider on his back for the first time in the confined space of a school or manège. However, if you have to do this in an open field, it is a good idea to fit the lunge rein as shown in the picture – that is, attached to the ring of the bit, taken over the head and through the ring of the bit on the near side. This is a safety precaution, in case the horse panics; should he do so, the trainer would not be able to stop the horse simply on a cavesson. As soon as you are happy that the horse is unlikely to panic, fit the rein on to the cavesson in the usual way.

leg over the back of the saddle, landing lightly in the saddle. You must take great care not to tickle or dig the horse in the ribs with your left foot as you mount, as this can easily upset a young horse and make him difficult to mount. Be careful not to drop your right foot onto the horse's rump when you take your right leg over his back. Carelessness can quickly upset any horse, so that you then have to take a lot of time and trouble restoring his confidence in you before you can progress much further. Always try to be aware of your actions, and do not take casual liberties with your young horse.

When the horse is gradually walking on the lunge, then he can be asked to trot for just a half-circle initially, with the rider in sitting trot. Once the horse is happy in trot then go rising, but this can be the moment when some horses become more aware of your moving in the saddle and get upset. The role of the person lunging the horse is vital. At this stage, the relationship between the lunger and the horse is more important than that between rider and horse, because the horse so far only has real confidence in the lunger. As you progress with the rider to walking and trotting on both reins ridden, and making transitions from walk to trot and vice versa, then the rider will slowly take over the control of the horse from the person lunging.

If, on the other hand, the rider is not very experienced, it may be a good idea to change roles at this stage, so that the less experienced person becomes the lunger, while the more experienced person is now the rider, in order to give the horse more confidence and to take on his further training.

THE POSITION OF THE RIDER: THE SEAT

The correct seat is carefully described in every book on equitation. The seat and balance of the rider are most important factors, for without being in control of your seat you cannot control or be in harmony with the horse in movement.

Firstly, consider sitting in the lowest part of the saddle with your weight evenly distributed on both seat bones. Your legs hang naturally round the curve of the horse's body with a slight bend of the knee. The foot rests in the stirrup with the ankle supple, the feet facing forward. The body is upright and straight when viewed from behind, and when viewed from the side there should be a vertical line running through the ear, shoulder, hip and heel. This position remains constant for all paces, but as the horse moves there is considerable movement which must be absorbed by the rider's body. Only when the rider is supple enough in the waist can he sit to the movement of the horse.

You must pay particular attention to the following aspects of your position on the horse.

The Back
This must be upright and straight, allowing of course for the natural curvature of the spine.

The Waist and Lumbar Area
This is the part of your body which absorbs the mobility of the horse, and it must be carefully controlled, and used in the right way. The hip bones should be slightly forward, with the lumbar vertebrae showing a curve forward before joining the more rigid thoracic vertebrae. This is where many riders lack suppleness, and any tension in this area will cause bumping against the movement of the horse, creating discomfort for horse and rider.

The Shoulders
These should be of equal height, with the shoulderblades laid flat against the back of the ribs, so that the upper arm hangs down in the natural position. The elbow should be bent and flexible, to allow the hand to follow the movement of the horse's head. The hands should be carried in front of the rider with the thumbs uppermost, the fingers closed and the wrist very slightly bent. Any stiffening of arms or shoulders results in the elbow taking

The correct seat and position of rider in the saddle. There should be a line through the rider's ear, shoulder and hip to the heel. The elbow should be bent and there should be a straight line from the elbow, through the hand to the bit. The legs hang down naturally, the calves folding round the horse's sides and the toes are up, the heels down. The rider sits evenly on both seat-bones, the upper body upright, not slumped, and looks straight ahead.

Exercises while riding on the lunge. (*Opposite*) Correctly performed, these can help to improve a rider's position, suppleness and balance, as well as giving him a good feel for the horse's movements. The trainer controls the horse, so the rider can concentrate wholly on the exercise, and on maintaining his position and balance.
I The rider keeps his feet in the stirrups and holds on to the pommel with one hand. He lifts the other arm and swings it

up an unnatural position, and causes resistance in the horse.

The Head

The head should be upright, with the rider looking ahead. The neck must be straight, not allowing the head to poke forward.

Once the horse is in motion the rider must think of controlling and maintaining a constant position on the horse. His legs must go down and fold round the horse so that they are correctly placed to give the signals to the horse. The body must not be slumped on the horse, but carried with the diaphragm firm. You cannot expect to have a horse in perfect balance if you are not sitting in an erect and upright way. If you walk like a ballet dancer then you may be able to ride in an elegant manner. Perfecting one's seat takes years of training, and few riders pay enough attention to disciplining themselves before taking on the training of a young horse.

THE MOOD OF THE RIDER

Many other factors also affect your performance as a rider. Sometimes one can become stiff or tense for no apparent reason, or because of outside circumstances, such as being overtired or worried. You must then decide either

1

2

3

4

backwards in a circle. The exercise which helps to loosen the shoulders, should then be repeated with the other arm.
2 No longer holding on to the pommel at all, the rider raises both arms to shoulder level, concentrating on keeping his balance and an upright position. He then swings the arms forwards and backwards alternately. This helps to loosen the waist and upper body.
3 The trainer has changed the rein; all exercises should be done going in both directions. Now the rider has no stirrups and has raised both arms to shoulder level. He will swing them in rotary movement backwards, again maintaining the correct position and balance with the horse on the circle.
4 The rider is in the normal riding position, with no stirrups, holding his hands as if he were holding the reins (which in fact he is not doing). He is sitting correctly, balancing with the motion of the working trot.

to loosen yourself up with exercises and put your worries aside, or to go and do something else. I have also noticed that children have good days, when they are receptive and teachable, and bad days, when they are unable to ride effectively. I can remember feeling the same myself. Sometimes one becomes really enthused and everything goes well – you sit well, feel well and the horse goes well. Then, at other times, you do not get that feeling and depression sets in, especially with the young. It is important not to allow this depression to linger, but to go and do something else like hacking out in the woods, or gymnastic work such as jumping or working over trotting poles. The rider is helped to progress, the horse works well, and both horse and rider are given a change.

THE AIDS OR SIGNALS GIVEN TO THE HORSE

The aids are the horseman's way of expressing his wishes to the horse, and the more experienced the rider the more refined the aids become, to the point of being almost invisible to the onlooker but clearly understood by the horse. The horse too must be carefully taught how to interpret the aids, by the rider repeating the action and ceasing it as soon as a response is felt and understood.

There are two types of aids.
■ The Natural Aids: the rider's seat, legs, hands and voice.
■ The Artificial Aids: the whip, spur, and any form of martingale or third rein.

When giving **leg aids**, pressure is applied on or behind the girth. If the horse is being ridden in a straight line, pressure on the girth is used to activate the inside hind leg and to maintain the forward momentum.

When asking for sideways movement or a bend, the inside leg is held on the girth more passively.

THE NATURAL AIDS

The natural aids are described here first, in the order in which you use them: seat, legs, then hands.

The Seat Aids

These are very slight movements of hip joint and pelvis, and are used mostly in conjunction with the legs.

The seat is used as a driving seat when the rider slightly alters the angle of the pelvis to tip forwards a little, lifting weight slightly for more impulsion or forward energy.

The seat is used more deeply, but with the body erect and the legs lengthened, to create greater energy and collection, so the horse is rebounding off the ground with the hind legs more fully engaged.

Unilateral use of the seat. This is when you move one seat bone slightly forward to influence the direction of the horse's hind legs, such as in shoulder-in work.

Weight transfer. This is when slightly more weight is on one seat bone than the other, for example when moving into canter, or in some lateral work.

The Leg Aids

Leg aids ask the horse to move forward, activate his hind legs, and indicate direction.

By using both legs just behind the girth you ask the horse to move forward. The leg is used with little vibrations, not the large kicks which are sometimes seen demonstrated by ignorant riders. Because the horse's natural reaction is to move away from anything it does not understand or is frightened by, so its natural reaction is to move forward from the legs when they are closed around him.

When the leg is not being used, it is passive but lightly closed round the horse in the correct position.

The leg held passively **behind the girth** in a forward movement supports the hind legs and prevents the horse from deviating to the side. When it is closed more actively against the horse's side in this position, it asks for forwards and sideways movement.

HOLDING SNAFFLE REINS

1 Looking down, it can be seen that the reins pass up through the hands and are pressed on to the first finger by the thumbs.

2 Seen from the side, the rein passes between the third and fourth fingers, and up through the hand.

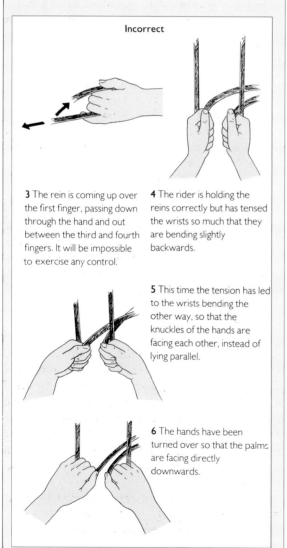

Incorrect

3 The rein is coming up over the first finger, passing down through the hand and out between the third and fourth fingers. It will be impossible to exercise any control.

4 The rider is holding the reins correctly but has tensed the wrists so much that they are bending slightly backwards.

5 This time the tension has led to the wrists bending the other way, so that the knuckles of the hands are facing each other, instead of lying parallel.

6 The hands have been turned over so that the palms are facing directly downwards.

HOLDING THE REINS OF A DOUBLE BRIDLE

1 The snaffle reins pass beneath the little fingers of each hand, and the curb reins between the third and fourth fingers. Both reins then pass up through the hands together and are held against the first fingers by the thumbs. This is the most common way to hold the reins of a double bridle.

2 The curb reins pass beneath the little fingers, and the snaffle reins between the third and fourth fingers. This method is used when the rider wants greater control of the curb reins.

3 Both curb reins and the snaffle rein from one side are held in one hand, whilst the other hand holds only the snaffle rein. This method is much favoured by riders from the Spanish Riding School; it allows the rider to use mainly the snaffle rein.

4 The curb reins pass beneath the little fingers of each hand, and the snaffle reins are held between the first finger and thumb. This is a method often used with horses who tend to lean on the rein too much.

The Hand Aids

The hands contain the impulsion created by seat and legs, control the speed, indicate direction, and help with seat and legs to balance the horse.

The hands take hold of the reins and, through the bit, indicate to the horse's brain your wishes. They should never be used alone, but always with the leg, or seat and leg, preceding their use. Just as you cannot steer a car until it is in gear and going forward, so it is with a horse.

The hands should be independent of the action of any other part of your body, and should remain still in relation to the movement of the horse. There should always be a light but elastic feel in your hands and wrists, indicating to the horse that he can be allowed more rein if needed. The fingers should be closed lightly round the rein which, if a single rein, should pass from the bit between third and fourth fingers, and come out through the top of your hand with your thumb resting on top of the rein. The feeling you have, and the tension on the rein, should be as light as possible, and it is up to you to teach the horse the contact which is acceptable to you both.

The Individual Use of the Hands

Most horses are naturally slightly crooked, so you have to teach them to take an even feel on both reins. Some never fully achieve this, but you must ride them forward and keep trying to indicate the correct tension by taking a contact on the 'soft' side of the horse, and releasing the stronger side.

When riding, one talks about the inside and outside hand in relation to the direction one is riding around the arena. In this sense, you ride the horse with the seat and inside leg on the outside hand which maintains a steady contact and controls the speed and balance of the horse. The outside leg helps to keep the horse straight.

The inside hand accepts the bend which is created by the rider's seat and leg aids. The hand aid should be light and flexible, and able to direct the horse round corners or circles. When riding in straight lines one still rides the horse forward slightly, thinking of an inside and an outside hand, so that you have a positive rein to ride the horse into.

The Voice

This is an important way of controlling the horse, especially in his early days. The voice is used to soothe and praise the horse, to encourage him to move forward, and to correct him. By sharp use of your voice the horse soon learns to 'Walk on', 'Trot', and later 'Canter' on the lunge, just as he learns from your soothing tones to 'Trot', 'Walk' and 'Whoa'. Some people use 'Halt' as a command, but I

know I would only say 'Whoa' when my horse is panicking, so this is how I train them. The horse learns 'Good boy' for when he has done well, just as a sharp look in the eye and a growl reprimand him.

THE ARTIFICIAL AIDS

The Whip

This is an aid used to reinforce the leg, should the leg be insufficient. The schooling whip, used for schooling on the flat, is about a metre (three feet) long and should be used without taking the hand off the rein. This whip should just touch the horse, or if necessary flick him, behind the leg, should he be lazy or not understand the leg. When there is a response to the whip it should be followed up by some praise, so that the horse learns to understand why the whip has been used. The whip can be used in either hand.

The Spur

Used in a similar way to the whip, the spur reinforces the leg aid or refines the use of the leg. The spur is used in a stroking action, and should be used only intermittently and when required to create extra impulsion. When the spur is fitted, the rider must be able to use the leg without the spur touching the horse.

The Martingale or Third Rein

These reins or straps should not be necessary in training the dressage horse, but sometimes a standing martingale attached to the noseband is a help with a young, nervous horse when he is first being ridden. The running rein can be used for older horses who have been spoilt, but for all experienced riders these should not be necessary.

Natural and Artificial Aids — The Right Balance

If a rider is relying too heavily on the artificial aids, it usually means that the natural aids are being used incorrectly. This may be due to a poor seat or a lack of balance on the part of the rider, so always correct yourself before blaming the horse. Properly used, the whip and spur refine the natural aids; used wrongly, they can have the opposite effect. Any confusion over the aids can cause grave problems for the future, so time must be taken to re-establish understanding before attempting further progress.

Refining the aids is a never-ending process for the dressage rider, as he progresses from the early stages to the more advanced movements considered in the following chapters.

CHAPTER FOUR

PACES AND TRANSITIONS

THE TROT

■

THE HALF-HALT

■

THE WALK

■

THE CANTER

■

TRANSITIONS OF PACE

When ridden training of a dressage horse begins, he must be taught to
execute his natural paces correctly – that is, in balance and harmony –
as is clearly being achieved in the **trot**. He must also learn to
change from one pace to another with the same smoothness and grace.

USING THE *MANÈGE*

When it comes to the training and riding of the horse, a study of his paces and transitions is important. One must also make sure one is using the *manège* correctly. A *manège* is usually either 40×20 metres (44×22 yards) or 60×20 metres (66×22 yards), which is the International Equestrian Federation size. The size is not as important as using the corners of the *manège* correctly. Riding circles which are round, controlling the horse's quarters and

shoulders throughout the movement, and keeping his balance, are the main areas we must look for when schooling and riding in the *manège*.

(Right) **David Hunt riding Maple Zenith** in the beautiful setting of Blenheim Palace. The dressage arena in front of the house, seen here, is well laid out, with the

markers clearly and correctly spaced. The flowers around the arena add a touch of colour to the proceedings.

The dressage arena
Competitions at Medium level and above are held in the larger sized arena. It is of great benefit to practise in a large arena, both for advanced movements, and also in the early stages when training a big

young horse, in order to give him more space. As the horse becomes more balanced and controlled, he can be asked to perform movements in the smaller arena.

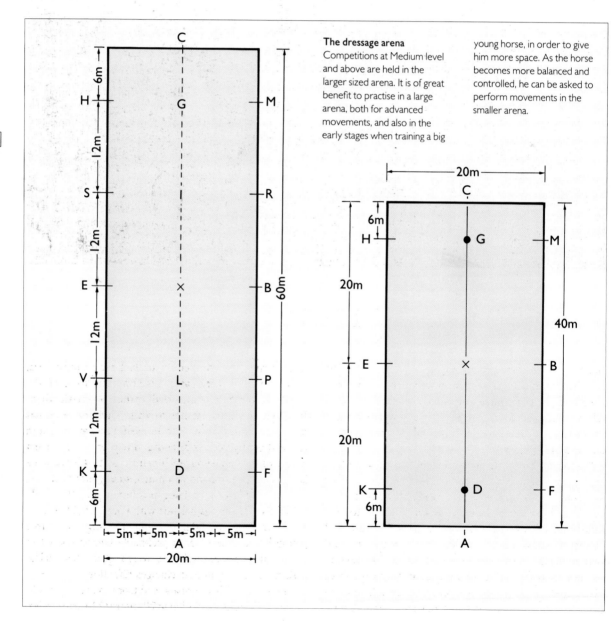

THE TROT

Our study of the horse's paces begins with the trot, for this is the pace with natural impulsion, at which one works a horse initially. (Of course you must allow the horse to walk on a long rein for at least five minutes when you first mount, to allow his muscles to relax and loosen up, before starting serious work.)

The trot is a two-time movement, with the horse's legs moving in diagonal pairs, separated by a moment of suspension. Some horses have a good natural rhythm in the trot, and each stride feels strong and powerful to ride. Unfortunately, other horses lack this natural rhythm, and the suspension is nearly lost when the horses hurry and are tense. This can sometimes occur when the horse first has the weight of the rider on his back and is incapable of balancing himself. Or the rider may have been hurried in his lunge training and failed to establish the horse's paces.

Alternatively, the horse could just lack action and natural ability. In all of these cases it is important to teach the horse to move quietly and slowly in the trot – so slowly, in fact, that he almost wishes to walk. Then, once he has stopped running away with himself, you can ride him forward gently with your seat and legs into the correct rhythm. Every time you feel him hurry so that his balance falls on to his forehand too much, steady him until you feel you are in the driving position again, then ride forward and keep his balance with your upright seat.

The trot can be ridden in rising or sitting trot. With a young horse, rising trot is preferable because it is less tiring, but the rider must be sure to change the diagonal he is rising on every time he changes direction.

The horse with an unbalanced trot requires time and patience. He must be ridden in 20-metre (22-yard) circles, and once the rhythm is established, he can then go large round the manège, still ridden in the same balance. Gradually, changes of direction can be introduced, such as serpentines, turns and smaller circles.

The horse with a naturally good rhythm and balance is quicker and easier to go on with, but one must remember that his swing and elasticity can be used against you. Care must be taken to make sure his energy is used in the correct way. The impulsion from the hind legs must become used to taking the weight of the horse, as well as propel the horse forward. The rider must learn to feel this and adjust the horse accordingly. These horses should be asked to go into the corners of the manège to help engage the hind legs. Then an increase in the length of stride can be introduced for a few steps, and next, through the half-halt, the horse should respond to the downward transition by bringing the hind legs more under him, until he is back in his own carriage.

THE AIDS FOR THE TROT

- Sit evenly on both seat-bones, in an upright position.
- Close both lower legs gently round the horse.
- Move body in unison with horse's movement.
- Control forward impulsion lightly with the reins.

Working trot

1 Hind legs are active and well under the horse.
2 He is moving with forward, swinging steps.
3 The back is swinging gently in rhythm with the movement.
4 The nose is slightly behind the vertical. This should be corrected by the rider balancing the horse and allowing a little more rein when he is correctly balanced.

Collected trot

1 Hind legs are very active and well bent.

2 The hindquarter joints are well bent, showing acute angle, so as to bring the impulsion well under the rider.

3 The steps are higher and shorter than in other trot paces.

4 The forehand is lighter and the neck slightly more arched.

5 The head is on the vertical line, with the jaw relaxed.

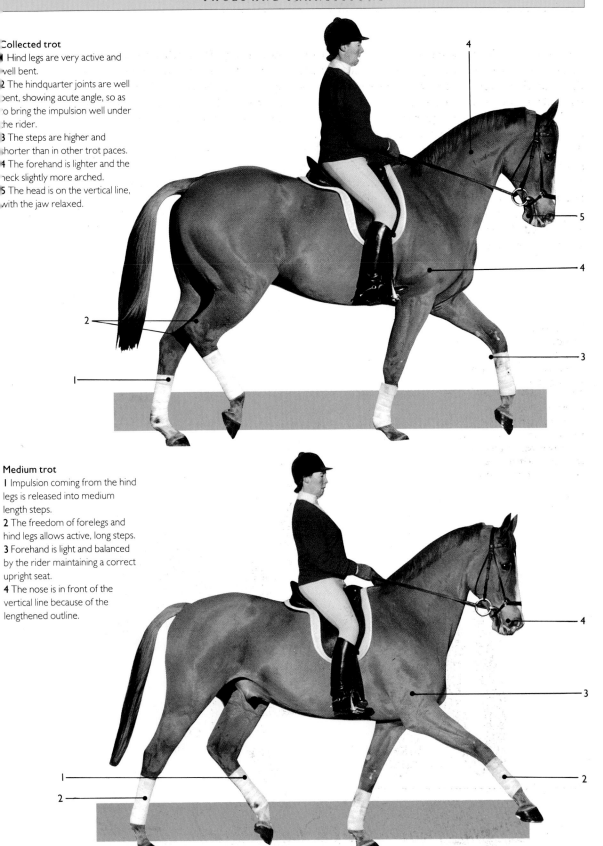

Medium trot

1 Impulsion coming from the hind legs is released into medium length steps.

2 The freedom of forelegs and hind legs allows active, long steps.

3 Forehand is light and balanced by the rider maintaining a correct upright seat.

4 The nose is in front of the vertical line because of the lengthened outline.

Extended trot
1 Hind and forelegs are equally active. Line of cannon bones is directly parallel in diagonal legs.
2 Outline is lengthened to maximum without loss of balance.
3 Nose now a little more in front of the vertical, to allow for the full extension of the steps.

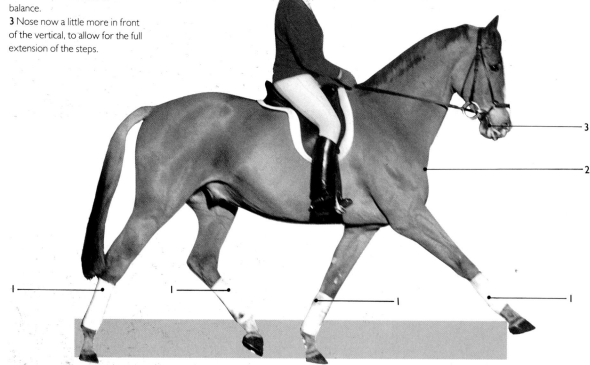

COMMON FAULTS IN THE TROT: CAUSES AND CURES

■ In working trot, horse is running forward. Not in self-carriage, he is falling on to the forehand and becoming overbent.
■ Too much pressure in reins. Half-halt to regain balance, then take up correct outline.

■ Horse is on forehand, his hind leg is behind the line of the foreleg and is 'dwelling'. He is overbent.
■ Too much weight in the reins. Rider's hands should 'give' a little.

■ Horse is in medium trot – too much on the forehand, and not in self-carriage. Right foreleg is too high and toe is flicking upwards.
■ Too much pressure in the reins: lighten contact slightly.

Transition from medium trot through half-halt to collected trot
1 Here the rider has slightly straightened her back and lightened her seat to ask for a half-halt. She is using her seat, legs and hands to indicate a request for the transition from medium trot.

2 The horse has responded and has decreased his speed and length of stride.

3 The rider has asked for another small half-halt to gain more collection, which the horse is already showing by the heightening and rounding of the steps.

4 From the half-halt, the horse is now in collected trot. The rider has released the half-halt aids, and is indicating that she wants the horse to stay in this pace. Note the correct bending of hocks and knees, and good outline of the horse's frame.

THE HALF-HALT

The half-halt is an important part of riding and must be taught to the horse early. It is a way of asking the horse to rebalance himself and also to listen to the rider before asking him to do any movement. First you half-halt, then you give the aid for the movement.

When teaching the half-halt you correct your position, close your lower legs and gently push the horse into a restraining hand until the horse engages his hind legs. You lighten your seat a fraction and allow with the hand as soon as you feel the response of the horse, using his hind legs to slow himself. You then ride forward again at the original pace, or alternatively ask for some movement. Sometimes it is beneficial to use repetition and association of place to help you teach the horse what you require in the half-halt. With a young horse, start in walk, and turn across the school, for example, asking for halt across the centre line. Repeat this perhaps 20 times, until the horse is beginning to anticipate your wishes and almost halting for himself, then ride forward again. You can then change into trot and ask for transition down to walk using your voice as well as legs, seat and hands. Then, when the horse is responding to the downward transition, but before he changes into the lower pace, prevent this by using your seat and leg aids to ride forward again. When this is achieved in the same place, and you feel the horse understands your aids for the half-halt across the centre line, go on to practise the half-halt in different parts of the manège, until you can ride in trot and perform several half-halts with the horse listening to your aids. The half-halt should then be practised in all paces, as the horse becomes better balanced with its use.

Once the half-halt is well established, the transitions within the pace are not too difficult to achieve. It is very important not to allow the horse to run in the lengthened strides. If this happens, he must be asked to half-halt; then try again for just a few steps. As the horse's balance improves, the number of steps can be increased until he is in a correct balance throughout the length of the manège.

When one starts working the young horse, as we have seen, he should be ridden in working trot. This is an active trot with the horse's impulsion coming from his hind legs. The horse will maintain his balance and be steadily controlled between the rider's legs, seat and hands. A horse who is in correct balance and self-carriage can move in medium or extended trot all round the manège without

losing rhythm or cadence, and with a half-halt he will come back to collected trot, moving with softness into the shorter and higher steps demanded from collection.

From the working trot, medium trot, collected trot and extended trot can be executed. Working trot into medium trot is the natural progression forward, and when this transition has been established, then a collected trot must be obtained before a real extended trot can be expected. For it is only from true collection that a full extended trot can be achieved. In extended trot the horse is activated from the hind legs, the forehand is light and free, and the horse has freedom to use all his limbs fully to his maximum power, without losing his balance.

THE AIDS FOR THE HALF-HALT

- ■ Sit in correct upright position.
- ■ Close lower legs into a restraining but allowing hand.
- ■ Lighten the seat.
- ■ Close leg again, and allow with hands as horse responds.
- ■ Apply aids for next movement required, or to stay in current pace.

The half-halt
1 Rider's seat erect and upright.
2 Lower legs applied gently against horse's sides.
3 Hands restraining but allowing.
4 Horse is attentive.
5 Hind joints are well engaged.
6 Steps are shortened and heightened.

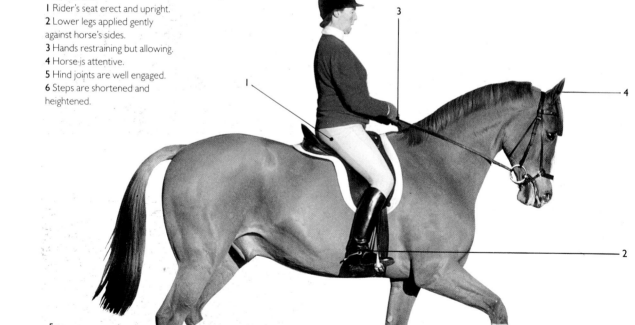

1

2

3

4

Half-halt in canter

1 The horse is in working canter along the long side of the arena. Note the length of his outline, and the easy, relaxed stride.

2 The rider has lightened her seat and closed her legs, pushing the horse forward into a restraining but allowing hand. You can see from the horse's head and the swish of his tail that he is listening to the command.

3 He has responded to the aids by heightening and shortening his steps – note the higher action of the off fore. His outline is more compressed and rounded, as he has 'concertina'd' his body.

4 The rider has released the aids for the half-halt, and the horse is now going forward in his own balance, staying light on the forehand.

5 In the next step, in collected canter, he is in perfect balance, still light on the forehand and moving forward on the track.

5

Exercises for the half-halt

1 Perform a serpentine in walk down the manège, asking for a full halt at each point marked X. After each halt, either walk or trot to the next point. Asking for a full halt will instil in the horse the idea of listening to the rider and checking before a change of pace.

2 Begin in trot and make wider loops of a serpentine down the arena. Change the pace at X's from trot to walk, then back to trot, to walk, to trot, and finally back to walk, to complete the serpentine.

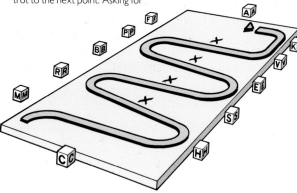

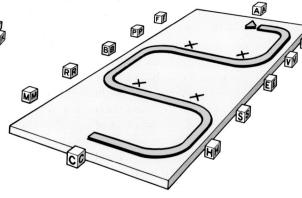

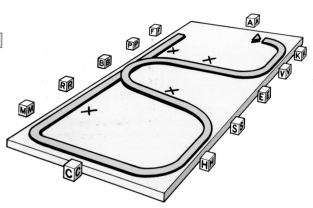

3 The whole of this exercise is conducted at the trot. Ask for a half-halt at the points indicated, but then trot on again, rather than changing the pace. After the serpentine, ride down the long side of the manège, asking for two half-halts.

THE WALK

The walk may be considered next, because it is a pace which is often used in the rest period given after work in trot.

The walk is a four-time pace, when four hoof-beats should be heard; there is no moment of suspension, and each of the steps should be of the same length. You should be able to count each foot-fall, and the beat should be the same. The sequence is: left hind leg, left foreleg, right hind leg, right foreleg. There are four different types of walk: free walk on a long rein, medium, collected, and extended. The walk is the most difficult pace to obtain collection from, and is the easiest pace to destroy. Faults at the walk frequently develop from incorrect riding. There is little impulsion in the walk, due to the slowness of the pace, and often the horse is pushed out of his natural beat by the rider hurrying the steps, or pushing the horse into too strong a rein.

When riding a young horse, the walk is used to relax the horse and is only walked on a long rein. When the horse has worked in trot, he may be given plenty of rest periods in walk on a long, loose rein as reward and relaxation after the stronger work. As the horse learns to accept the rider's aids, gradually the long-rein walk is compressed into a medium walk, when the horse is activated into lively forward steps remaining 'on the bit'. The hind feet should overtrack the front feet in medium walk. In the collected walk the strides are shorter and higher, the horse has a lively impulsion from the hind legs, the forehand is light, and the horse remains on the bit with his outline appearing shorter and rounder. In extended walk, the steps should be as long as possible, the horse remaining on the bit but with a longer and lower outline. The steps should not be hurried and the overtracking of the hind legs should be to the maximum.

The rider should always be aware of how the horse moves in walk, and allow the horse to use his head and neck. However, the horse must respond to the aids and the rider should gradually teach the horse to listen to the aids, so that when the rider applies the legs and pushes the impulsion into the reins, the horse responds by containing the energy, ready for whatever is required by the rider. If the horse has a naturally poor walk and does not overtrack with the hind legs, it is often caused by lack of swing in the back and neck. In this case, it is probably best to work the horse well in trot and canter so that he is tired, before working on improving the walk. After the horse has worked he will want to lower and lengthen his neck and this is the time to ride plenty of small serpentines in walk, constantly asking the horse to go forward on to the rein and allowing him to take the rein

THE AIDS FOR THE WALK

- ■ Sit on both seat-bones evenly and lightly.
- ■ Control horse with seat, leg and reins into the correct rhythm of the movement. The length of stride and balance required will depend on whether collected, medium or extended walk is requested.

Medium walk
1 Impulsion contained between rider's seat, legs and hands.
2 Outline slightly compressed.
3 Hind legs overtrack foreleg steps.
4 Horse lightly accepts the bit – his nose is in front of the vertical.

Extended walk
1 Steps are long and swinging, covering maximum ground.
2 Outline is stretched forward to maximum.
3 Horse is still accepting the bit – his nose is in front of the vertical.

forward. By constantly changing direction, you encourage the outside hind leg to swing well forward, and then the horse learns to gradually swing in his back and lengthen the steps.

There are other problems related to the walk – for example, some horses constantly hold back behind the bit and just take short steps. This problem can be overcome by treatment similar to that described above for correcting lack of swing. Sometimes you may also need to touch the horse with the whip to make him take the rein, but if you do so and he jumps forward, you must be sure you do not then lose your balance and come back on to the reins suddenly, thus punishing him with the reins. When the horse is moving forward on to the contact, a lot of practice at going from walk to trot and vice versa is important, so that the horse responds to your forward riding aids as soon as he is in walk. Indicate to him the allowing hand, and try never to be restricting. Another problem is the horse who paces or ambles at the walk. This occurs when the walk becomes a two-time pace, with the near and off legs moving laterally. To achieve this, the

horse stiffens his back and usually raises his head. In such cases, it is important that the horse should be pushed into the contact so that he takes the rein and lowers his head, and the speed of the walk must be kept very slow, until you can hear and feel the walk becoming a four-time pace again. Pacing usually starts with the rider asking for too much speed in the walk, and hurrying the horse out of his natural rhythm. Horses with very long strides in walk are the ones which are especially easy to spoil: the rider may feel the horse is lacking impulsion because the stride appears so slow, and then break the stride by trying to quicken it. The walk is the last pace to ask for real collection in so do not be in a hurry.

COMMON FAULTS IN THE WALK: CAUSES AND CURES

■ Horse inattentive and not listening to rider, so is above the bit and out of balance.

■ Correct with more lower leg, and a little half-halt to balance him and ask him to listen.

■ Horse is on forehand and overbent. He has taken too much pressure on the reins, moving the rider off her seat.

■ Correct with lower leg and seat to bring horse into correct line.

Collected walk
1 Steps are shorter and rounder.
2 Joints more active to give springy steps.
3 Outline more compressed.
4 Nose close to the vertical.

THE CANTER

The canter is a pace most horses find easy, but there are some who are very unbalanced, and can canter only at great speed!

The canter is a three-time pace with a moment of suspension. The horse is said to be in 'right canter' when the right foreleg is leading, and in 'left canter' when the left foreleg is leading. The sequence when in left canter is right hind leg, left hind leg and right foreleg together, left foreleg, then a moment of suspension before the next stride begins. The canter should be established at a working pace with even strides, active hind legs, and a good balance and outline, with the horse remaining steadily on the bit and going straight. The horse must always canter with impulsion and rhythm. The head and neck work in co-ordination with the body, as the horse moves over his leading leg. When both his hind legs are off the ground, his head and forehand are momentarily lower. During the moment of suspension his body levels off, the next hind leg hits the ground and his forehand and head and neck are higher. It is during this moment of suspension that the rider indicates his wishes by correcting his seat and closing his legs in rhythm with the stride as he balances the horse.

The horse is disunited when the forelegs are on one lead and the hind legs are on the other lead. This is a most uncomfortable canter, and must be corrected immediately by bringing the horse back to walk or trot and starting canter again. A disunited canter is quite a common fault in young, unbalanced horses. Sometimes it is due to the horse losing his balance. On other occasions, it may be due to the rider asking for too much inside bend, or to the horse being very stiff and unbalanced, and not ready to canter with the rider until he is better balanced in trot. With difficult cases, it may be helpful to go into a field where you have plenty of room and no sharp corners, and ride the horse well forward in canter. The horse must

Medium canter
1 Hind legs are active, resulting in long steps.
2 Shoulders are free and mobile.
3 Forehand is light.
4 Nose in front of the vertical.

learn the aids for canter right and left, and the rider must make these clear when teaching the young horse. The aids for left canter are: first, establish sitting trot, if rising, then ask for a little half-halt. Apply the leg aids, which are right leg used behind the girth, left leg on the girth, slightly lighten the left seat-bone, and indicate a slight left bend. In the early stages, use your voice to help, and even the whip if necessary. The correct canter lead should be established immediately with an experienced rider in the saddle, as he can feel when is the correct time in the trot stride to ask the horse for the strike off. With a kind word as his reward for doing the correct strike off, a horse quickly learns the canter aids. It is then up to the rider through the sympathetic use of his seat and legs to make sure that the canter becomes balanced and rhythmical. From the established working canter, the horse can be asked to lengthen his stride for some steps, and then to shorten them again. The length of stride must come from the impulsion created by the hind legs, with the horse remaining steadily on the bit. When the horse is really coming through from behind, the steps will grow or shorten very smoothly. From the lengthened strides, you can ask for medium canter; then, with a half-halt, go back to working canter. Turns and circles can help work in canter, provided the horse is kept balanced and ridden forward. Transitions from canter to trot, and trot to canter, must be practised until they become easy for the horse, and from this one can progress to more direct transitions, such as walk to canter. However, transitions really require a section to themselves!

THE AIDS FOR CANTER LEFT

- Half-halt.
- Left leg on the girth.
- Left seat-bone slightly forward.
- Right leg behind the girth.
- Left rein asks for slight flexion to left.
- Right rein controls the shoulders and keeps the horse's balance.

Working canter
1 Active steps from all legs.
2 Freedom of shoulder allows free, energetic steps.
3 Weight is slightly on forehand.
4 Nose in front of the vertical.

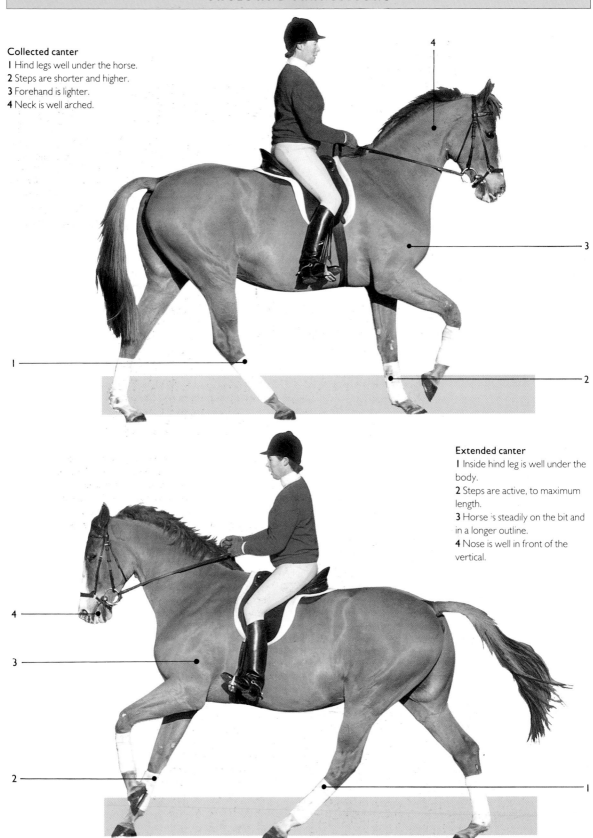

Collected canter

1 Hind legs well under the horse.
2 Steps are shorter and higher.
3 Forehand is lighter.
4 Neck is well arched.

Extended canter

1 Inside hind leg is well under the body.
2 Steps are active, to maximum length.
3 Horse is steadily on the bit and in a longer outline.
4 Nose is well in front of the vertical.

Medium canter
1 A good example of a horse going forward well and happily in medium canter. This first illustration shows him in the moment of suspension in the canter stride.

2 The rider keeps the horse moving forward in the rhythm of the pace by using her seat and outside leg. The inside leg remains on the girth to maintain the slight bend to the left. The horse has taken the next step in canter sequence, and has his near hind and off fore on the ground.

3 In this next step – most of the weight is now on the near fore – it can be seen that the medium canter is a good, swinging pace. It comes between extended and working canter, and may be seen as a preparatory pace for full extension.

4 Now the horse has completed one full stride, and is back at the moment of suspension again. The illustration shows clearly how all four feet are well clear of the ground – another indication of the freedom and springiness of the pace. Throughout the stride, the rider has maintained a light contact with the horse's mouth, allowing him freedom for his head to move in rhythm with the pace.

A FAULTY TRANSITION TO CANTER

1

2

3

4

5

1 The horse is resisting the half-halt request, putting his hindquarters to the inside of the track, tightening his back and neck, and 2 coming above the bit. 3 In the next stride, he is making the transition into canter very rough, preparing to buck, and 4 kicking out with his hind legs.

5 Some measure of harmony is restored and the horse is now in right canter. The rider is a little stiff, making the horse overbent.

TRANSITIONS

The transition from walk to canter is best started near a corner of the arena. First walk the horse well into the hand, half-halt a little, then apply the canter aids, keeping the balance throughout the transition. The transition from canter to walk is a little more difficult, and at first can be progressive through trot. Before asking for the transition, several half-halts must be made, then ask for walk and allow it. Over a period of several weeks the horse will become progressively more balanced and able to perform the movement directly. After a time, you will be able to start on the simple change.

THE SIMPLE CHANGE

This is a movement when you start in, for example, canter left; go from canter to walk; and, in either one or three strides of walk, move forward directly into canter right. This is a simple change, and initiates the horse in some form of collection for both the upward and downward transitions. Sometimes you may encounter the problem of the horse tightening his back and resisting the downward transition by resisting the hand. This can often be overcome by doing the transition during a turn. Care must also be taken to stop the horse anticipating the movement, so sometimes walk must be established for at least a 20-meter circle before asking for canter. At other times, the horse may drop the bit and come behind the leg, so that you cannot ride forward without the horse

coming behind or above the bit. This can be helped by riding forward into a strong working trot, or riding forward into a 10-meter circle as you go forward to canter, and then riding the horse with strong legs into a firmer contact before lightening to the correct contact again. One problem which may arise at this stage is that of the horse getting a four-time canter. This occurs when the second beat in the stride is slightly broken because the diagonal pair of legs are not touching the ground together. It is usually caused by lack of jump in the hind legs, and may be related to the horse being ridden with

---

THE AIDS FOR SIMPLE CHANGE – FROM RIGHT TO LEFT CANTER

- ■ Correct position in the saddle.
- ■ Half-halt back to trot.
- ■ Allow trot for two steps.
- ■ Apply aids for left canter:
    Left leg on girth
    Left seat-bone slightly forward
    Right leg behind girth
    Keep left flexion
    Right rein maintains straightness and balance.
- ■ Keep horse moving forward in canter on this leg.

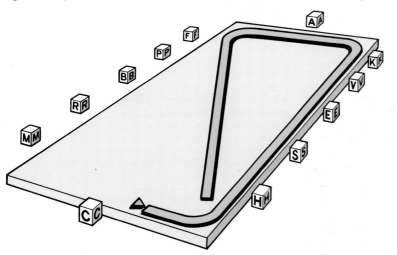

Lengthening the stride in trot and canter
In either working trot or canter, ask for lengthened strides down the long side of the arena, return to working pace across the short side, then change the diagonal. Ask again for lengthened strides down the second long side of the arena; shorten the stride for a few paces half-way along (Marker B or E), then lengthen stride again. The alternate lengthening and shortening of the stride helps to increase the horse's collection.

The simple change – canter to trot, back to canter

1 Here the horse is listening to the aids he has been given for a half-halt in the canter, and has balanced himself for the downward transition.

2 He is slightly running on to his forehand, but is still in canter.

3 Now he is performing the first trot step which is active and true.

4 The horse is listening to the canter transition aid being given by the rider – her left leg on the girth, her right leg behind the girth. This has been preceded by a half-halt.

5 He is performing the first step in canter, still listening to the aids.

6 Now in the second step of the canter, he is happy and confident he has performed the movement required.

too much restriction in the rein and insufficient activation from the legs. If this happens, you must ride the horse more forward, asking for really strong, pushing strides from the hind legs. It is usually easier to activate the horse on a large circle, and a touch with the whip for a few strides will help to activate the hind legs. If the horse bucks or kicks at the whip, he must be reprimanded and taught that the hind legs must come forward when touched with the whip, and not the reverse. Only when you have restored the canter to a true working canter can you think of slowing the speed a little once more, but, in doing so, make sure you ride the correct rhythm with your seat and legs. Slow down only for a short spell, then ride forward into medium canter and repeat this several times, so that the horse is expecting to be ridden forward, then the true canter will be restored.

Always remember to correct your own position and aids whenever you encounter a problem, for often these are caused simply by a lack of carriage on the part of the rider. Once the working and medium canter are well established, the collected and extended paces can be worked on — but these will be dealt with in the next chapter.

COUNTER CANTER

Counter canter may be introduced once the horse has a good balance in his canter work, is able to increase and decrease the pace, and shows early collection. Accurate riding, using the corners to the full, is essential to gain the maximum benefit from the movement in the training of your horse.

Counter canter is taught in the early stages by means of canter loops in from the track. Initially, a loop of 3 meters

Exercises for the simple change
1 Begin teaching a horse the simple change on a serpentine movement; as his introduction to the half-halt was on a serpentine, he will be ready to check at the same points. Canter a left-handed loop, ask for walk as you cross the arena, and then give the aids for right canter. Canter round the end of the arena and come back to walk as you go across the diagonal.

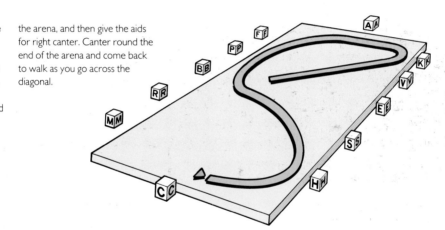

2 Using the diagonals. Begin on the long diagonal in walk, ask for right canter at the end of arena, then turn on to the short diagonal, ask for a few steps of walk, and go into left canter. Change the direction, walk again, and then go into right canter. These exercises all relate back to the training for the half-halt, but eventually the horse must learn to do simple changes anywhere in the arena.

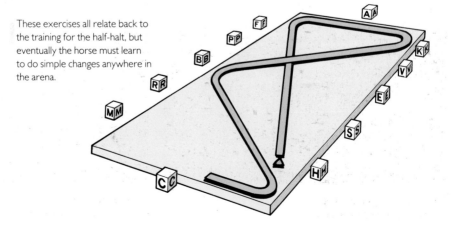

in from the track, over the marker E or B, is sufficient. As the horse's balance improves, 5 meter and 10 meter loops may then be ridden. The rider should take the horse in a soft curve, making sure that he retains control of the horse through the outside rein as he leaves the track. If outside rein control is lost, the rider's weight will fall on to the horse's outside shoulder, so that the horse will become unbalanced, and probably lapse into a disunited canter. When riding counter canter correctly, the horse should have a very slight flexion in the leading leg.

Once the horse can perform a canter loop of 5 meters, a little more collection will be required to perform a balanced canter loop of 10 meters. When this is established, the horse is ready to perform a true counter canter, in which he can canter right round the arena on both the left and the right rein. Riding true canter and counter canter with simple changes round the arena, and then on a 20 meter circle, can be a useful preparation for teaching the horse flying changes (see page 96).

The counter-canter loop
1 Left leg on girth
2 Right leg behind girth.
3 Left seat-bone slightly forward.
4 Left rein keeps slight flexion to left.
5 Right rein keeps balance and helps direction.
6 Left (leading) foreleg about to hit the ground.

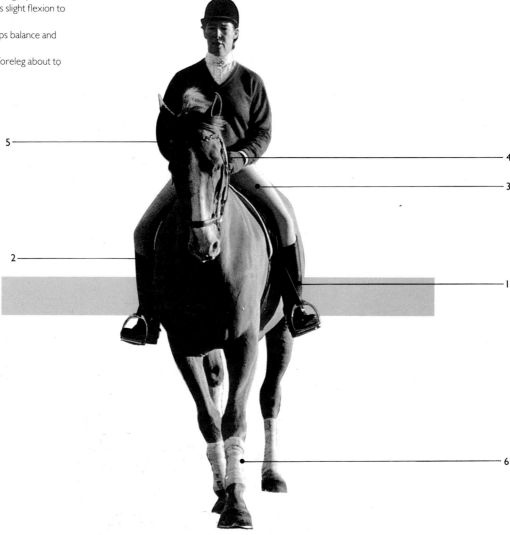

1

2

3

4

5

6

Riding a 5-metre loop in from the track

1 In working canter, the horse is ridden well into the corner, then balanced with a half-halt.
2 The rider directs the horse off the track and then across the diagonal.

3 The horse is coming off the track -- the rider is keeping the left flexion and riding him straight forward.
4 This is the moment of turn to make the loop. The rider keeps her right leg well behind the girth and holds the horse between the reins, directing him in the new direction back towards the track. The left seat-bone should be forward.

5 As the horse changes direction, the rider must control his balance and rhythm with both lower legs.
6 The rider rides straight forward, going well into the next corner, keeping the horse balanced in canter on the track.

CHAPTER FIVE

WORKING TOWARDS COLLECTION

COLLECTION AND EXTENSION

THE HALT AND REIN-BACK

INITIAL LATERAL WORK

SHOULDER-IN

Lengthening and shortening of the stride and horse's outline to achieve extension and collection are important lessons in dressage training. At the same time, the horse can be introduced to lateral work – that is, moving forward and sideways, as shown in the **shoulder-in,** performed here at the canter.

INITIAL COLLECTION AND EXTENSION

By the time the horse has progressed through his initial paces of walk, trot and canter, both horse and rider should be well balanced. Once the horse is able to go forward into a medium pace and back to a working pace in both trot and canter, he should be ready to start taking more weight on to his hind legs and can gradually be introduced to more collection.

In collection, the horse is expected to be at his most agile. His hind legs should give him plenty of impulsion. His steps should be higher and more mobile, with the joints of the hindquarters and hind legs well bent. The neck should be arched, with a continuous curve running from the withers to the poll. The head should be just in front of the vertical, which alters slightly throughout the step. The horse should have the potential energy of a coiled spring but without showing any sign of mental tension. As his training progresses, so the degree of collection and extension will increase. Without some collection, the horse cannot have true extension — the extended paces release the power pent up in collection.

In extension, the horse increases his length of stride to its fullest extent. He should remain calm and lightly on the bit. His head and neck should be slightly lowered and lengthened, so that his strides become longer and fully overtrack in walk and trot. His forehand should appear light and the steps unhurried. The unseen line of power comes from the hind legs, over his back and appears to go out through his mouth. In changing from extension to

The Rein-Back
1 Rider lightens the seat.
2 The lower legs are placed behind the girth.
3 Hands are gently restraining, but yielding with the steps.
4 The horse moves backward in two-time, taking diagonal steps.

THE AIDS FOR HALT AND REIN-BACK

- To halt, lighten the seat, close lower legs, and push horse forward into a restraining but allowing hand.
- As horse steps back, keep rein-aid light and slightly yielding with each step.
- After a few steps, halt, then close legs to ask for forward steps.
- Care must be taken not to hurry horse forward after a rein-back, because this can lead to anticipation and tension in the movement. Ask for a few seconds' halt, every now and then after a rein-back.

collection, the horse should pick up his feet to heighten each step and shorten its length. In this downward transition, the rider should not let the energy rush into the horse's shoulders but make him lower his hindquarters to keep control.

True collection and extension take considerable practice and cannot be perfected in the first lessons. The ultimate achievement in collection is teaching the horse to keep the energy in his hindquarters in the downward transitions; in extension it is teaching him to remain in self-carriage and fully balanced.

THE HALT AND REIN-BACK

When a horse becomes more obedient and responsive to the aids for both upward and downward transitions, the halt becomes easier to master.

THE HALT

Although a young horse soon learns to halt and stand still when asked, it is not until he is really accepting the aids that he can perform a true halt from walk or trot. In a correct halt, the weight of the horse should be distributed evenly on all four legs while he remains steadily on the bit and ready for movement forwards or backwards.

THE REIN-BACK

In the rein-back, the horse steps backwards with his legs moving in diagonal pairs. He should lift his feet well off the ground and not drag them backwards. His weight should be taken on his hind legs without any sinking in the back or lowering of the forehand. He should not resist the hand and should move backwards in a straight line. You must be careful not to ask a horse to rein back before he is sufficiently strong in his back and capable of a true halt. Once he has accomplished this, he should be asked to rein back by the rider slightly lightening his seat and closing the lower leg as if to move forward but, at the same time, restraining the forward movement with his hand. As soon as the horse steps back, he should be rewarded with praise and a lighter hand. No more than one or two steps should be asked for in the early stages.

Only when the horse is obedient to the aids should he be asked to step back. If he resists the rein aids, he must be pushed up with the lower leg and seat until he realizes that it is simultaneously a restraining but allowing hand. Do not overdo the rein-back, because the horse's back can become tired if it is practised for too long a period – a few steps each day is quite sufficient. After asking the horse to step back, ask him to walk forward again with light vibrating leg aids and an allowing hand. The horse must stay on the bit throughout.

Any tendency to run back out of control must be quickly but quietly corrected with forward driving aids and, if necessary, a touch of the whip. Running back is caused by a desire to drop the bit, so the movement should be ridden with slightly more leg aids and a light rein contact throughout. If the horse raises his head and hollows his back when asked for rein-back, then this should be corrected first. In this position, the horse cannot move backwards comfortably with the rider's weight on his back, so do not ask for rein-back until the horse has returned to the correct stance.

Care and patience is required in teaching the horse the rein-back. With some fine or Thoroughbred horses, the rider has to take a noticeable proportion of his weight off the horse's back and transfer some of it to his knee and thigh, although without leaning forward. In really difficult cases, it may be advisable to teach the horse the rein-back without the weight of the rider. This can be done using long reins, and once the movement is established, the rider can be re-introduced. This lesson must be learned over a period of time; in no circumstances should it be hurried.

If the horse does not move back in a straight line, this should be corrected with a little more pressure of the leg or rein aid on the side the hindquarters are moving out.

THE SCHAUKEL

When the horse has advanced in his training, then the rein-back schaukel can be performed. In this movement, the horse walks back a set number of steps, then immediately forwards for several steps, and then back again for another fixed number of steps. The legs should step back in diagonal pairs and should never be set down parallel to each other. The movement should be fluent, straight and harmonious, with the horse accepting the backward and forward aids without hesitation. This is a difficult movement for both the rider and horse to perform correctly, and it measures the horse's obedience and submissiveness.

1

2

3

4

5

Halt and Rein-Back

1 Here the horse is in a true halt, squarely placed, with his weight distributed over all four legs. He is on the bit and listening for the rider's next command.

2 Now he takes his first steps backward for the rein-back. Note how his legs are moving in diagonal pairs, and the steps are well raised.

3 Backward movement continues, now on the other diagonal, although the footfall is now not quite in two-time. The foreleg has come to the ground just before the hind leg.

4 Here the horse is in a better balance, taking a little more weight on the hind legs, so that the hind foot is now just about touching the ground at the same time as the foreleg.

5 He is about to complete the fourth step of the rein-back, after which he will be quietly ridden forward, perhaps after a pause.

INITIAL LATERAL WORK

When a rider has tested and trained his horse to respond to the aids and has him really balanced, keeping him straight and swinging through his back in all paces and transitions, then some lateral work may be started in order to help the collection and suppleness of the horse. Even in the earliest stages of riding, the horse should be taught to answer the leg by the rider using a stronger leg aid if the horse falls with his hindquarters to one side or the other. The rider should be constantly straightening the horse with the leg, seat and rein aids when he feels the horse's balance requires assistance. If this early training is performed correctly, moving into lateral work should not present any great problem. When a problem does arise, it is usually the fault of the rider, not the horse.

In lateral work, the horse moves forwards and sideways, with his hind legs on a different track from his forelegs. The horse is bent and flexed throughout his body in whichever direction the movement requires. There are three initial movements leading up to true lateral work. These are the turn on the forehand, the shoulder-fore and the leg-yielding. All three movements come into the early training of the horse, and help in loosening and straightening him.

THE TURN ON THE FOREHAND

This is a movement with little impulsion or forward motion, and is used to make the horse more supple and

Lateral bend
Before progressing to lateral movements, it is important that the horse should go forwards correctly, whether in a straight line, round a bend, or on a circle. The diagram on the left shows correct movement round a bend. The horse is bent evenly through his body, so his hind feet follow exactly in the tracks of his fore feet. This is achieved by the rider weighting the inside seat-bone and placing the inside leg on the girth for the horse to bend around, with the outside leg behind the girth to control the hindquarters. The inside rein asks gently for the bend, but is supported by the outside rein. In the right-hand diagram, the rider has not supported with the outside leg and rein, and in consequence the horse's hindquarters have fallen out of the track.

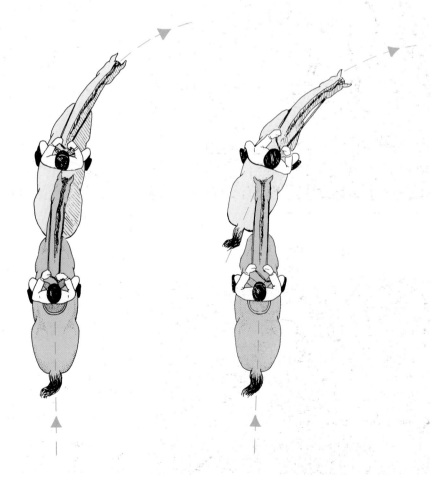

obedient to the sideways-driving aids. It is important when hacking out and is often practised when opening gates. In the turn on the forehand, the horse moves his hind legs round a half-circle while the forelegs stay as nearly as possible on the same spot. To perform the movement in the arena, you must ride about a meter in from the track, so that there is room for the horse to turn his head and neck. The horse is brought to a halt and, if moving away from the right leg, is flexed a little to the right with slight half-halt aids. The rider gently transfers his weight to the right seat bone, and his right leg gives quick vibrating movements behind the girth, pushing the horse's hindquarters in short steps sideways round the right pivoting foreleg. As soon as the horse responds, the rider applies a brief but firm pressure with his right leg. The horse's right hind leg should cross in front of the left hind leg until he is facing the other way. Throughout, the rider's left leg is held passively behind the girth to prevent the horse moving round too quickly and to keep him forward on to the bit.

If the horse does not respond or understand the leg aids, then the whip must be used gently with short flicks until he moves one step in the direction asked. He should then be praised. If the rider is quick and responsive he will soon teach the horse what is required; practising this movement early in a horse's training will make him a more manageable mount.

THE AIDS FOR THE TURN ON THE FOREHAND

- Half-halt.
- Apply left leg behind the girth.
- Apply right leg on the girth to maintain forward movement.
- Restrain gently with reins, but be ready to allow the movement.
- As horse moves away from left leg, apply seat and leg aids, in rhythm with the steps.
- Horse may be bent either way – either into the right hand, or bent to the left into the direction of the new movement.

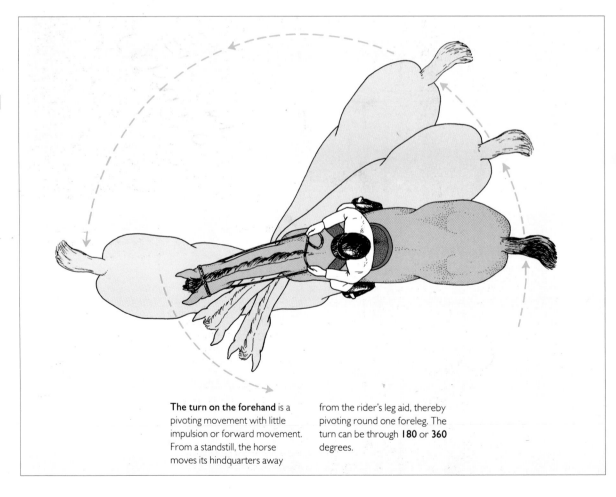

The turn on the forehand is a pivoting movement with little impulsion or forward movement. From a standstill, the horse moves its hindquarters away from the rider's leg aid, thereby pivoting round one foreleg. The turn can be through **180** or **360** degrees.

1

2

3

4

5

Turn on the Forehand

1 The horse moves away from the rider's left leg, stepping sideways to the right. The left hind leg is crossing in front of the right hind.

2 Here the left hind leg is clearly crossing in front of the right hind leg in the next step. The horse is contained between both reins and is kept moving forward with the outside leg.

3 Now the horse pivots round the left foreleg, while bent slightly to the left.

4 The right foreleg and left hind leg are moving to stop the pivoting movement as the horse changes direction.

5 After the movement, the rider asks the horse to move forward in a straight line.

INSIDE POSITION AND SHOULDER-FORE

These movements are used as a straightening exercise early in a horse's training. Horses are naturally narrower in the shoulders than in the hindquarters, and few move in a perfectly straight line especially when ridden in an arena. They know they are wider behind than in front so, if ridden close to a solid wall, they naturally protect themselves by moving with their hind legs slightly to the inside of each foreleg. Most horses are also born with a slight stiffness on one side. To maximize the horse's natural propulsion from the hindquarters, he must be kept straight, otherwise the energy goes out through one of his shoulders.

When riding in a straight line, the horse is said to be in position right or left, depending on which leg and rein contact is in control. Position right is used when riding on the right rein either on or off the track. The aids for position right are a forward-driving seat, the inside leg pushing the horse on to the outside rein which is restraining but allowing, and the inside rein keeping the horse straight and indicating direction. The inside hand should never pull backwards or across the withers, but should be held slightly away from the withers. When seen from above, the horse has a very slight bend towards the inside from head to tail.

To bring the shoulder-fore, or in from the track of the inside hind leg, the rider uses his inside leg to push the horse into a restraining outside rein. This activates the horse's hind leg, bringing it further underneath him. The outside rein then brings the shoulder in from the track, the inside rein indicating the bend. If viewed from the front, the horse's feet are on only three tracks showing the inside fore, the outside hind, and with the outside front obscuring the inside hind. When established in walk and trot, shoulder-fore is a very useful aid to straightening the horse in canter. It is also the basic exercise from which the shoulder-in is developed – this comes from greater collection, more bend and a slight increase in angle.

Shoulder-fore in canter
1 Seat and both legs ride horse forward in rhythm with his steps.
2 Left leg is placed on girth and pushes horse forward on to the right rein, bringing the shoulder in from the track.
3 Right leg prevents the hindquarters from falling out.
4 Left hand keeps a fractional bend.
5 Right rein controls horse's shoulders.
6 Left foreleg steps just inside left hind leg.
7 Right foreleg steps between both hind legs.

LEG-YIELDING

Another movement which helps supple the horse, making him loose and obedient to the sideways-driving aids, leg-yielding keeps the horse straight except for a slight inclination away from the direction in which he is travelling. The legs cross forward and sideways. For right leg-yielding, you should use forward-driving aids, a slight half-halt with a little more weight on the right seat bone, and the right leg just behind the girth to push the hindquarters sideways. The left rein should support the shoulder and keep the horse straight while the right rein indicates a right flexion. The left leg should support the horse and stop him running sideways away from the right leg.

Begin by riding the horse in leg-yielding either towards the wall of the arena, or as for shoulder-fore but without the bend. Alternatively, ride across part of the diagonal . When the horse is obedient and supple in this exercise, then the rider can practise leg-yielding away from the wall on the diagonal, going straight for a few steps, then changing the flexion and yielding back to the wall again. This is a good way to loosen the horse in his shoulder and stifle joints. The most common fault seen with leg-yielding is too much flexion, when the horse becomes bent and then falls on to his outside shoulder, so that the leg-yield becomes uncontrolled. This problem comes from too strong a rein aid and incorrect leg and seat aids. The rider must think principally of keeping the horse straight between both reins. The flexion should be the last adjustment made, and even then only a very slight one.

THE AIDS FOR LEG-YIELDING FROM THE LEFT LEG
- From a walk or trot, half-halt.
- Ride horse forward with seat.
- Apply left leg behind the girth.
- Apply right leg on the girth to prevent horse from falling sideways.
- Use right rein to control horse's shoulders.
- Indicate a slight flexion with the left rein.

Leg-yielding from the left leg
1 Seat rides horse forward.
2 Right leg keeps horse moving forward.
3 Left leg moves horse sideways.
4 Right rein controls horses's shoulder and prevents him from falling to the right.
5 Left rein asks for slight left flexion.
6 Legs move forward and sideways, in rhythm with steps.

COMMON FAULTS IN LEG-YIELDING: CAUSES AND CURES

- The horse is stepping forward and sideways, but he is falling on to the right shoulder and the flexion is becoming too great.
- The rider can correct this by putting her left leg further forward and riding more strongly with the right leg.
- Here the fault is accentuated even more, with the horse crossing too much sideways. The rider is sitting away from the movement by twisting her shoulders to the left.
- The horse must be straightened with the right leg and rein, and ridden more forward with the seat.

Exercises for Leg-Yielding

1 Ride a 10-meter circle at marker G, then leg-yield across the arena away from the circle to rejoin the track at K. Or turn down center line, leg-yield away from the direction of the turn at D to rejoin the track at B or M. Remember to use the outside rein to prevent the horse from falling sideways.

2 Turn the corner at the end of the arena and leg-yield away from the outside leg towards the center of the arena for a few steps. Ride straight for a few steps, then leg-yield back to the track and go straight. Leg-yield along the track, keeping the horse evenly balanced between both legs and reins.

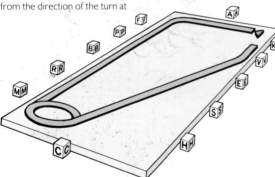

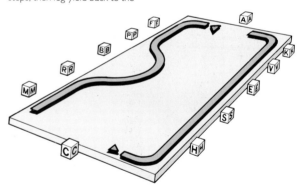

FURTHER LATERAL WORK: SHOULDER-IN

The shoulder-in is a movement that requires a certain amount of collection. The more a horse is capable of taking the weight on his hind legs, the lighter, freer and more mobile the forehand becomes. Shoulder-in is a very useful movement: it improves the collection of the horse, keeps him supple, and activates the inside hind leg. It also helps to make the horse accept both reins and keep a soft and relaxed jaw.

As with shoulder-fore, in shoulder-in only three feet are visible from the front, but there is more bend and collection in the movement. Since the horse is now more established in his work, stronger and more supple, he is

Shoulder-in left at canter

1 Rider looks between horse's ears.

2 Left seat-bone is slightly weighted.

3 Left leg placed close to the girth asks horse to bend and activates his inside hind leg.

4 Right leg supports and prevents the hind leg from falling out.

5 Right hand supports the shoulders, controls the bend, and keeps the balance.

6 Left hand indicates the left bend.

THE AIDS FOR SHOULDER-IN RIGHT

- Half-halt.
- Bring horse's shoulder in from the track, using the inside leg and rein, supported by the outside rein.
- Ride forward with the seat.
- Place outside leg just behind the girth to prevent the hindquarters from swinging out.
- Sit quietly throughout the movement.

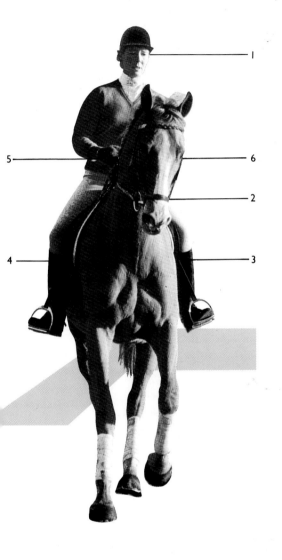

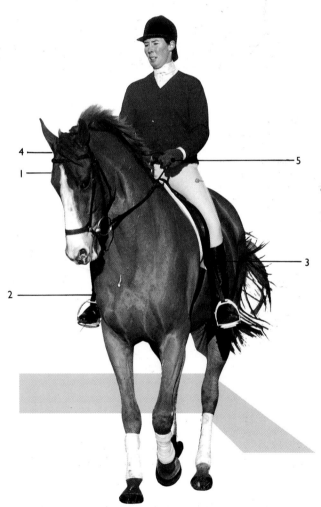

Shoulder-in right at trot

1 Right seat-bone is slightly weighted.

2 Right leg is placed on the girth.

3 Left leg supports the movement.

4 Right rein brings the shoulders in and keeps the bend.

5 Left rein supports the shoulders, controls the bend, and maintains the balance.

Shoulder-in

1 The shoulders are brought in from the track until the angle is approximately 35°. The outside fore and the inside hind are on one (the middle) track, while the outside hind and inside fore are on two separate tracks either side of this.

2 You can see here that the horse is slightly bent from his head to his tail round the rider's right leg.

1

2

3 The inside foreleg crosses in front of the outside foreleg, while the horse remains steadily in the bend.

4 As the inside hind and outside fore move forwards, so the inside hind is obscured by the outside foreleg.

3

4

able to show a greater bend both in his body and in the flexion of his knees and hocks.

The aids to shoulder-in are nearly the same as for shoulder-fore. First use the half-halt, then with the inside leg close to the girth, ask the horse to bend his body and step more forward and under with his inside hind leg. At the same time lead his shoulders in from the track with the inside rein while supporting the outside shoulder and keeping the horse's balance with the outside rein. The inside seat bone should be slightly more weighted, while the outside leg should be used behind the girth if the outside hind leg falls out, or if the horse tends to drop the shoulder out. The shoulder-in should be practised only for short distances to start with, but it is important to finish the movement correctly. A good exercise to help establish a correct finish is for the rider to bring the

horse's shoulder back to the track and to straighten him up using the outside rein and inside leg. Later, the rider can practise riding shoulder-in and going directly into a turn at the corner of the arena, or riding into a circle of eight or 10 meters and then continuing in shoulder-in. Shoulder-in also helps to activate the hind legs before asking for a medium trot across the half-diagonal.

Shoulder-in is a movement used daily in training and suppling every horse, however advanced he is in his education. When the movement has been established, it should be ridden on the center line or quarter line, and not always on the track. A horse feels a certain amount of support from the wall and so, if he is ridden away from it the rider is better able to check the horse's progress. Shoulder-in can also be ridden on the large circle and is a useful exercise for a horse who does not take an even

COMMON FAULTS IN SHOULDER-IN: CAUSES AND CURES

- The horse is resisting the rein and has too much bend in the neck. He is falling on to the outside shoulder – the outside rein not being in control. The rider must use more seat and legs, take more control of the outside rein and use less inside hand.
- The shoulder-in (*right*) is better, but the horse is very on the forehand, there is still not enough angle from the legs, and too much bend in the neck. Nor is there enough control from the seat and legs into the outside hand. There is too much initiation of the movement from the inside hand.

feel on both reins. In this instance, the rider must use much more outside leg to ensure that the hindquarters do not fall out.

A common fault in shoulder-in work is too much bend in the neck so that the shoulder falls out. This usually occurs when the horse is not sufficiently collected and the rider is depending on too much inside rein. The rider must correct this with a half-halt with both legs, using the outside rein to establish the balance. He should then ride the movement with a little less inside rein. Tilting the head is another problem which often arises. Too strong an outside rein is the cause and this can usually be rectified by the rider holding the horse in balance with more seat and legs and lightening the rein. If the inside rein is raised for a few steps, it corrects the tilt of the head and adjusts the bend so that the horse has a uniform curve of his whole body and neck.

When riding shoulder-in, one must constantly work for rhythm, swing and 'throughness' in the pace. If the rhythm changes greatly due to loss of impulsion, it must be corrected by the rider returning to circles or straight lines until it is properly re-established. The basic work of swing in the steps and elasticity of the back is of prime importance and must be constantly in the rider's mind. Any problems which occur with them must be corrected, however eager the rider may be to try the advanced movements dealt with in subsequent chapters.

Exercises for shoulder-in

1 Ride a 10-meter circle at marker H, then ask for shoulder-in down the track to E. Circle again and shoulder-in to K. Go straight round the corner, then turn and shoulder-in up the centre line .

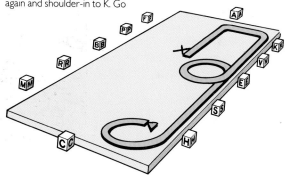

2 At H, do shoulder-in left to marker E, and then turn left. At marker B turn right, continue on round the arena to K. At K, ride shoulder-in right. Before you reach E, move forward in medium trot across the diagonal to M.

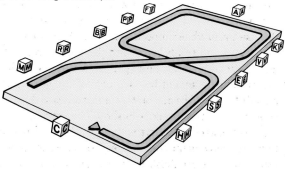

CHAPTER SIX

THE INTERMEDIATE STAGE

THE HALF-PASS

TRAVERS AND RENVERS

THE FLYING CHANGE

PIROUETTES

Once the principles of collection and extension have been learnt, and initial lateral work has been successfully achieved, more advanced lateral work can be undertaken. In the **half-pass,** illustrated here, the horse moves forward and sideways, bending evenly throughout his body in the direction of the movement.

THE HALF-PASS

Having achieved a high level of strength, suppleness and rapport with his rider in the earlier exercises, the horse is ready to pass on to the more complex movements of intermediate work. Now the rider can begin to work on the basic collection which has been obtained, with transitions which are ridden through with more power coming from the hind legs. At this stage, when the horse is obedient to the forward-driving aids, and fully in control when the sideways-driving aids are applied, he is ready to perform more demanding lateral movements, such as half-pass, travers and renvers.

In the half-pass the horse moves forward and sideways, bent throughout his body in the direction in which he is going. The horse's shoulders should fractionally lead his hindquarters and his outside legs cross in front of the inside legs. The half-pass can be ridden on a diagonal across the school, from the center line to the track or from the track to the center line. A 'counter-change of hand' is when the half-pass is ridden from the center line to the track and back to the center line or vice versa. The 'zigzag half-pass' comprises a series of half-passes performed down the center line.

The half-pass can be performed in all three paces, but in competitions it is seen only in collected trot and collected canter. The degree of sideways movement depends on the standard of collection, the training, the suppleness and the coordination of the horse. In early tests, the horse is asked to go 10 meters sideways over a 24 meters length, whereas at Intermediate standard and above he is asked to go 20 meters sideways over the same distance.

THE AIDS FOR HALF-PASS RIGHT

- From walk, trot or canter, ask for half-halt.
- Look in direction of movement.
- Apply right leg on girth for horse to bend around and to ride forward when required.
- Use right hand to ask for right flexion.
- Apply left leg behind girth for sideways movement.
- Use left rein to control pace and balance, and to regulate the bend.

Half Pass Left in Trot
1 The horse is showing a left bend, and is parallel to the side of the arena. His inside (left) leg is about to step to the left.

2 The outside (right) foreleg has crossed in front of the inside (left) foreleg. The horse is maintaining a good bend throughout the step.

3 Just fractionally later in the movement, and the hindquarters are slightly in the lead. As a result, the head is a little bit tilted. The rider must take her left hand a little more to left and ride forward with the left leg, supporting with the right rein to prevent the horse's right shoulder from falling out of line.

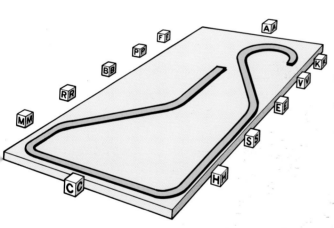

Exercises for half-pass
1 In any pace, ride down the track and do a half-circle to the center line. Ask for half-pass left towards E, or, if riding a young horse, half-pass to H to make the angle less oblique. Ride well into the corner of the arena and ask for half-pass right out of it to the center track.

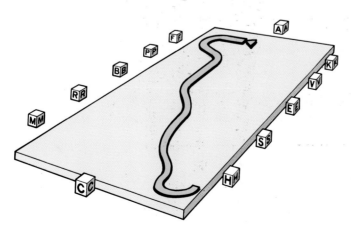

2 Half-pass and shoulder-in
Ride into the corner, then ask for a few steps in half-pass, followed by a few steps shoulder-in, working across the diagonal to the opposite corner of the arena. This is a good exercise to make sure the horse is correctly bent round the inside leg. Again, it can be executed in any pace.

THE AIDS FOR HALF-PASS

Ridden from the second corner of the short side of a school to the centre line, the aids for half-pass are as follows. Before the corner, half-halt, ride well into the corner with the inside leg and ask for a good bend and flexion to the inside. When the horse's shoulders are positioned on the diagonal, slightly weight the inside seat bone and allow the inside leg to become passive but forward-driving, with the outside leg asking the horse to move sideways. Take great care not to use the outside leg prematurely because this makes the horse bring his quarters over too soon, resulting in the quarters leading the forehand. This problem can be prevented by the rider taking one or two steps in shoulder-in before asking for the half-pass. As the rider becomes more co-ordinated with the aids, the horse becomes better balanced in the half-pass. The amount of impulsion created with the inside leg depends very much on the individual horse, but he must be given an inside leg to bend around. All too often riders forget the correct aids and the half-pass resembles an incorrect leg-yield.

The correct rhythm must always be paramount in the rider's mind when riding half-pass, and any loss of pace must immediately be corrected. If the horse shortens his steps, then the half-pass must be ridden more forward, less sideways, with the rider concentrating on the bend and allowing the quarters to trail slightly until the horse can keep his balance and rhythm. He can then be asked to step under the rider and move more sideways as his collection improves. When riding a young horse in half-pass, the bend is often apt to be lost after several steps. This can usually be helped by riding in a circle or riding straight into shoulder-in for a few steps then repeating the half-pass.

COUNTER-CHANGE OF HAND

When the horse is fully established in half-pass, then a counter-change of hand can be ridden. In this movement, it is important that the quarters are brought completely straight in the last step. The horse is given one or two straight steps to prepare for the change of bend and flexion, then ridden in the new half-pass. Only when this change-over is successfully accomplished can the zigzag half-pass be attempted, in which you are aiming to make a completely fluent change from one direction to the other with the straight steps becoming minimal. The zigzag requires great co-ordination of the rider's aids.

COMMON FAULTS IN HALF-PASS: CAUSES AND CURES

- The horse is moving sideways nicely, but his quarters are trailing a little, and he is slightly on the forehand. The rider is tipping her shoulders and sitting against the movement.
- The rider can correct the faults by looking more towards the direction of movement and using a little more left leg to correct the quarters.

- Here the actual step of the half-pass is very good, but the horse has moved sideways at quite a strong angle, which is perhaps too much for his capability as yet, and has caused him to tip his nose.
- The rider can correct the fault by riding more into the left rein to lessen the angle, then lightening both reins to balance the movement.

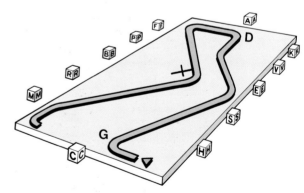

Exercises for counter-change of hand
Starting from the corner, turn down the centre line at G, half-pass right to E, then change the bend, half-pass left to D, go straight and turn left.

Or, ride into the corner of the arena, then half-pass to X. Go straight for a few strides, then change the bend and half-pass out to M. Ride into the corner.

TRAVERS AND RENVERS

Travers and renvers are movements in which the horse's body is bent in the direction of motion. In travers, the hindquarters are brought in from the track with the horse bent around the rider's inside leg. In renvers, the shoulders are brought in from the track and the horse is bent around the rider's outside leg. Viewed from the front, the angle is greater than that of shoulder-in, so four feet are seen, not three. Travers and renvers are more demanding than shoulder-in and often used with other gymnastic exercises such as shoulder-in and half-pass.

TRAVERS

The aids for travers down the long side of the arena are as follows. Before the corner, half-halt, then ride into the corner with the inside seat and leg. As you come out, allow the inside leg to become more passive while the outside leg, placed well behind the girth, asks the horse to move sideways. The inside hand should keep the flexion, with the outside hand regulating the bend and maintaining the balance of the horse. The inside leg should be placed at the girth to give the horse stability, and used more strongly only if the horse's hindquarters come in too much.

Like shoulder-in, travers should sometimes be ridden on the center line, and in fact it is a useful movement when ridden in conjunction with shoulder-in. A good exercise is to ride the horse in shoulder-in, followed by an eight or 10-meter circle, a travers, and then a half-circle and half-pass. These movements flow well together and help to establish a positive bend throughout the horse's body, giving him the opportunity to achieve real balance and rhythm.

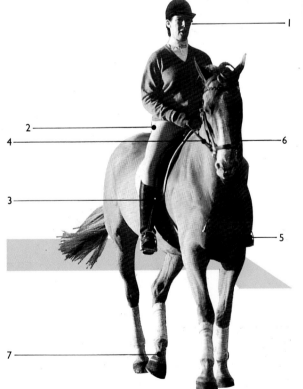

> **THE AIDS FOR TRAVERS**
>
> - Half-halt just before corner of arena.
> - Ride horse into movement with a light seat.
> - Apply right leg on girth for horse to bend around, and to ride forward into movement.
> - Use right rein to ask for right flexion.
> - Apply left leg behind girth to move the hindquarters into the movement.
> - Use left rein to control balance and regulate bend.

Travers

1 Rider looks ahead in the direction of the movement.
2 Rider's seat is used firmly but lightly to ride horse forward into the movement.
3 Inside (right) leg is placed on the girth asking for the inside bend, and also riding horse forward into the movement.
4 Right rein asks for inside (right) flexion.
5 Outside (left) leg is placed behind the girth to move the hindquarters into the movement.
6 Left rein controls the balance and regulates the bend.
7 Horse's outside (left) hind leg moves forward and under the horse to cross in front of the right hind leg.

Riding Travers in Trot
1 You can see clearly in these pictures that the travers is a four-track movement. Here the outside hind and inside forelegs are on the ground, with the horse well bent throughout his body.

2 Because the horse's weight is on the inside hind leg and outside foreleg, the bend through the body appears much greater. In fact, this is an illusion brought about by the placement of weight.

3 Here you can see clearly how the outside hind leg is brought forward and under the horse to step in front of the inside hind leg.

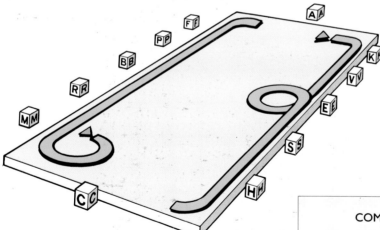

Exercises for travers
Travers is often performed down the center line, but these movements are useful for training. 1 Ride the horse out of the corner and ask for shoulder-in, then do an 8- or 10-meter circle to rejoin the track and ask for travers.
Alternatively 2, ride an 8-meter circle at one corner, then ask for travers down the track.

COMMON FAULTS IN TRAVERS: CAUSES AND CURES

■ The horse has his hindquarters in from the track.
■ Horse is not bent correctly – his body is straight and only his neck is slightly bent.
■ Rider should place the inside leg on the girth for the horse to bend around.
■ She should sit straighter and use much less outside leg – the inside leg has been forgotten.

RENVERS

Renvers is, perhaps, a more difficult movement to achieve than travers, because the rider has to position the shoulders and then ask for the bend when riding it on the track. It is, in fact, easier to ride renvers down the center line, especially if coming out of a 10-meter circle, as you hold the hindquarters on the center line, while keeping the shoulders and bend beyond it.

The aids for renvers are as follows. Half-halt at the three-quarter point of the circle, slightly weighting the inside seat bone. Place the inside leg passively on the girth, using the outside leg behind the girth to drive the horse forward and round the inside leg. The hands should regulate the bend in the direction of the movement. Keep the horse forward and on the line with the inside leg.

To ride renvers on the track, start as if riding shoulder-in, then change the bend to the direction of motion by weighting the other seat bone and changing the flexion and bend. Renvers is a useful exercise to perform when a horse is reluctant to finish the half-pass. Ride the half-pass nearly to the track, keeping the bend and the hindquarters pushed over on to the track and take renvers on for several steps. The sequence half-pass, renvers, a reverse half-circle and half-pass again (see diagram on next page) is a useful exercise to establish and reinforce the correct bend throughout all these movements.

THE AIDS FOR RENVERS

- ■ Half-halt.
- ■ Use right rein to bring horse's shoulders in from the track.
- ■ Apply left leg on the girth for horse to bend around.
- ■ Apply right leg behind girth to keep hindquarters on the track.
- ■ Use left rein to ask for left flexion while right rein maintains balance and control of the shoulder.

Renvers
1 Rider looks in the direction of the movement.
2 Left leg is on the girth for the horse to bend around.
3 Left hand asks for left flexion.
4 Right leg is placed behind the girth.
5 Right hand controls the shoulders and the bend, and balances the movement.

Riding renvers in trot
I The horse has just come round the corner of the arena and the rider is asking for left flexion for the **renvers**. The horse is pictured almost in the moment of suspension in trot.

2 The horse has established the bend and angle of the renvers. The outside (left) hind leg is being placed just in front of the inside (right) hind leg, and the inside (right) foreleg is crossing in front of the outside (left) foreleg.

3 The inside (right) hind leg and outside (left) foreleg are being brought forward and under the horse.

Exercises for shoulder-in and renvers
I Begin with shoulder-in (then half-pass) across the arena, leading into renvers to rejoin the track. Or 2, half-pass and renvers: come out of the corner in half-pass, at the track go into renvers, ending with a reverse half-circle. You could go into half-pass again after this, if you wish.

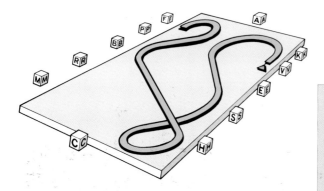

THE COUNTER-CANTER

This exercise is an important part of training the horse in canter, and one that requires balance, obedience and collection. The horse canters round the arena with the outside leg leading either in a circle or straight lines. A horse that is correctly trained and obedient to the canter aids should find this movement easy. The counter-canter and the simple change — see Chapter 4, p. 67 — should both be practised before attempting the flying change.

THE AIDS FOR COUNTER-CANTER RIGHT ON A LEFT TRACK

- Ride around arena in working or collected canter, with outside leg leading.
- Use seat to ride horse forward and keep him balanced.
- Just before a corner, half-halt to balance horse, so he can negotiate corner in counter-canter.
- Keep right leg on girth to ride horse forward and help him bend slightly to right.
- Keep left leg behind girth to indicate right canter.
- Use right rein to control and keep flexion towards leading leg.
- Use left rein to balance and direct horse around corners, or to keep him on circle.

The Counter-Canter

1 Rider's seat helps ride the horse forward and keeps him balanced.

2 Right leg is kept on the girth to ride the horse forward and help him bend slightly to the right.

3 Left leg is placed behind the girth to indicate the right canter.

4 Right rein controls and keeps the flexion towards the leading leg of the canter.

5 Left rein balances and directs the horse around corners, or keeps him on a circle.

Counter-Canter Right

1 The horse moves in right canter, negotiating a left-handed corner. His body is slightly bent towards the leading leg. The rider's left leg is firmly behind the girth, while the left rein is keeping the balance and speed of the canter.

2 Now he is on a straight line in counter-canter, in the second step of the canter stride, with diagonal legs coming to the ground. He is showing a nicely balanced outline.

3 The rider is asking for a half-halt by placing her left leg a little further back and raising the diaphragm, while using her seat to push the hind legs a little more under the horse to balance him for the next corner.

Exercises for counter-canter
1 Canter left-handed round the arena in true canter. Immediately after the corner, canter off the track in a 3-metre loop. This loop is then in counter-canter. Increase the loop to 5 metres, then 10 metres, so that the counter-

canter is more pronounced. In a 60 × 20-metre arena, you can lead into a serpentine movement.

2 Begin with a half-circle in right canter, rejoin the track at B, now in counter-canter. Make a three-quarter circle back to X, then canter right in a half-circle to rejoin the track. Stay in right canter throughout the exercise.

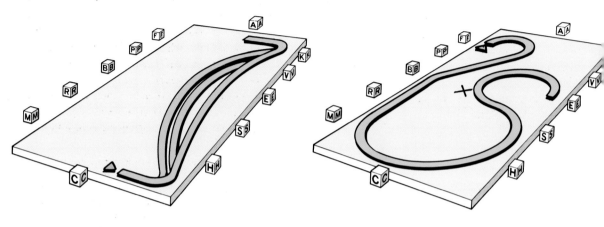

THE FLYING CHANGE

The flying change is a natural pace when the horse jumps from one canter leading leg to the other during the moment of suspension in the canter. Horses with very good active canters find the flying change very easy to execute. Horses lacking jump in the canter will find it more difficult because the moment of suspension is lacking. You are aiming to achieve lightness and expression in the flying change, and for this you need a canter which is collected, active, straight and springy.

THE AIDS FOR THE FLYING CHANGE

To execute this movement well, the rider must be able to feel the exact moment to ask for the change. He must make sure he has his legs correctly positioned closely round the horse, and, because the change takes place at the moment of suspension, the rider must give the horse sufficient warning.

A preparatory half-halt is important to get the horse to listen to the correct aids for a flying change. Move the original outside leg forward just before asking for a change with the new outside leg, which moves back with stronger contact behind the girth. The seat rides the horse on while allowing him to jump, the new inside seat being pushed slightly forward. The legs can then ride the horse forward and straight or give a half-halt if required. The

flexion is minimal and is used only to keep the forehand straight. There should be no flexion to the new inside leg, contrary to common belief. The reins are used only to keep the balance and to give support.

COMMON FAULTS

It is important to keep the change straight from the start: swinging the hindquarters is a bad fault and will affect a horse's later training. A high croup is another fault which must be corrected early in the horse's education: this can turn into a major problem and is an evasion of the aids.

THE AIDS FOR FLYING CHANGE

- In right canter, ask for half-halt.
- Release left leg slightly forward.
- Move right leg back behind girth to pick horse up and place him in left canter.
- Ride horse forward with seat, but lighten it slightly at the moment of change.
- Use hands to control shoulders, balance and speed.
- Place left leg on girth to keep canter rhythm and activate steps.

who changes with a high croup, begin by several half-halts, then change with plenty of freedom, riding forward during the actual jump. The rider may have to give a half-halt soon after the change because, while correcting the balance of the change itself, he may have lost balance generally. The flying change aid must be given quietly but firmly — any throwing of the rider's weight upsets the horse's balance and makes it more difficult for him.

It is easy for a horse to become upset with careless riding of the flying change. The rider must be sure to keep balance and straightness while releasing the new inside leg sufficiently early not to confuse the horse. If the horse increases his speed into the change it is likely that the change will be late behind. In this case, more collection is needed. Working on a circle with transitions from counter-canter to true canter with simple changes can help eradicate this fault.

TEACHING THE FLYING CHANGE

When teaching a horse the flying change, using a *manège* can be an advantage. Changing the rein on the short diagonal and asking for the change before arriving at B or E is a good place to start. Alternatively, ride a canter half-pass to the track and, when fully straightened up, the horse will be ready and well balanced for a flying change. Make sure you ask for the movement well after the half-pass or anticipating could creep in. When the horse fully understands the aids and is happy and settled performing the flying changes while changing the rein and other

Flying change: Right canter to left canter

1 Left leg is released forward a little.
2 Right leg moves back behind the girth.
3 Rider's seat rides the horse forward, but is slightly lightened at the moment of the change.
4 Hands control the horse's shoulders, balance and speed.
5 Left leg is placed on the girth to keep the canter rhythm, but allows the left hind leg to jump through to make the change.

The Flying Change
1 Before making the change, the rider has asked for a half-halt to make the horse pay attention. You can tell by his ears that he is listening for the next instruction.

2 The horse has just performed the flying change. The rider has lightened her seat slightly to allow the horse to jump into the air to make the change.

3 The horse has landed on the left leg, and is now in the second stride of the canter. The rider allows him to go forward, while maintaining the left canter position.

Exercises for flying change
These exercises are useful for teaching horses the flying change.
I In left canter, leave the track and ride a 20-meter half-circle: ask for a flying change at point marked X in the diagram. Circle to the right to rejoin track.

2 Circle from the track in right canter, then ask for a flying change at point marked X, and circle to the left. Ask for another change at the lower point marked X, and half-circle again. Intersperse these exercises with asking for flying changes down the sides or quarter line, and across the diagonal.

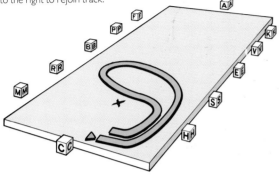

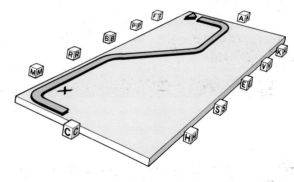

variations, then practise off the track, changing to counter-canter and then back to true canter. At this stage, the counter-change of hand can be practised in canter but the rider must always make sure the horse is straight before asking for the change.

The rider must take time to build up collection throughout the whole training of the horse before teaching the canter pirouette. Transitions in canter are an important part of establishing the required collection. Ride in working canter with many transitions to collected canter. Next, give a few half-halts in collected canter, always checking the horse's straightness by riding in a position right or left. Then ride forward to working canter again. These transitions can be practised on a large circle, on the diagonal, or anywhere on the track. Some steps riding in shoulder-fore in canter help to activate the inside hind leg of the horse; then, from this, the large canter half-pirouette can be asked for. The rider's chief concern must be the correctness of the steps and the balance of the horse — not the size of the pirouette. Any tendency to throw the shoulders round must be corrected with the outside rein and inside leg, and the pirouette made larger. Once a large half-pirouette can be performed with the horse in balance, the rider can practise a circle with the horse bent in the direction of the pirouette. Ride travers on the circle, then make a correct circle and ask for a few steps of smaller pirouette, and so on until the horse can accept the collection and balance.

Correct pirouettes are obtained through careful training and not from forced riding. Horses that are short coupled and with a naturally good canter pace find the pirouette easier than a large long-backed horse. Any

Exercises for half-pass and flying change
Cantering right-handed, turn down the centre line, then half-pass out to the track. Canter straight for a few strides, then ask for a flying change at point marked X. This is a very good exercise, because the horse will be well collected with his hind legs really under him in the half-pass, and with good right flexion.

tendency for the horse to raise the forehand and come above the bit in little jumps on the hind legs should be corrected by riding the horse strongly with the legs into the hand and making him come into canter with more energy from the hind legs. Some flexing of the neck before riding the pirouette can help to loosen the horse.

Work should not become too repetitious. Changing the pirouette sometimes to a half-pirouette, a three-quarter pirouette, or even two pirouettes makes the horse listen to the aids. However, never overdo the practice of the pirouette on any one day.

When the horse is in true collection and balance, the rider can begin to aim for the correct size of pirouette — although even with a highly-trained horse the perfect pirouette is achieved only occasionally. Usually, the horse is capable of performing the movement if he is correctly muscled and fit, but it is the rider who needs so much practice in collecting and balancing the horse and in using the aids correctly. Every horse is different, and one may need more inside or outside leg and seat than another. It is this 'feel' and sense of timing a good rider develops which is so important when riding advanced dressage.

THE HALF-PIROUETTE

The half-pirouette is a 180° turn when the horse steps around the inside hind leg without stopping, his body flexed in the direction of the movement. When correctly performed, the inside hind leg takes the most weight, with the forefeet and outside hind foot stepping round the inside hind foot. It is vital that the horse maintains the correct sequence of steps, whether in walk or in canter. The inside hind foot is raised and put down almost in the same place, or forming the smallest possible half-circle. The aids for the half-pirouette are as follows. After a preliminary half-halt to increase the collection, the inside hand gives the flexion and indication of direction. At the same time, the outside hand allows the horse forward while limiting the bend and controlling the shoulder. Weight the inside seat bone slightly, activate the inside hind leg with a vibrating inside leg, and control the haunches with the outside leg behind the girth. It often helps to use the inside and outside legs alternately. A half-halt will have to be performed during the actual turn if the horse is losing his balance or moving round too quickly.

THE WALK PIROUETTE

In the walk pirouette, it is important to keep the steps active and forward, even if the movement is too big. As the horse becomes more collected, then the steps of the half-pirouette are ridden to the correct size. Always keep the bend in the direction you are going. After the exercise is completed, the horse should be ridden forward in a straight line.

You must be confident that you are in control of the pirouette at all times and can test this by riding out of the movement. The inside leg and outside rein stop the pirouette but the rider must be careful to be in time with the steps of the horse and not to hurry him on to the straight line.

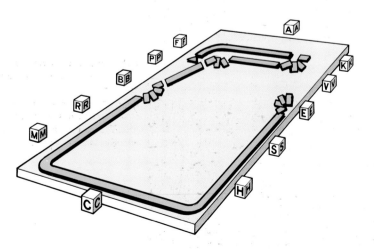

Exercises for walk half-pirouette
Walk round the manège asking for half-pirouettes at intervals.

1

2

Pirouette in walk

1 The horse is ridden along the track in collected walk. The rider asks for a half-halt and indicates right flexion. Her right leg is placed on the girth to activate the inside hind leg. The left leg controls the quarters. The right rein keeps the bend, while the left rein controls the shoulders and the bend.
2 The walk sequence is maintained. The hind legs are still active and that activity is maintained by the inside leg vibrating near the girth.

3

4

3 The left foreleg steps in front of the right foreleg as he begins to make the pirouette turn.
4 Now at almost 90° to the track, he continues the pirouette with active steps.

5

6

5 The bend is maintained throughout the movement. The horse is coming back towards the track, to face the opposite direction.
6 In the final steps of the pirouette, the rider maintains the right flexion as the horse's forehand nears the track. She keeps the quarters under control with the left leg behind the girth.

7

8

7 The horse is about to rejoin the track with his forehand. The rider is still maintaining the bend.
8 The rider releases her left leg and rides forward on the track at the same walking pace. The horse remains on the bit throughout the movement.

THE CANTER PIROUETTE

In canter pirouette, which can be either a 180° or a whole 360° turn, the horse is bent in the direction of motion with very collected, high steps. The quarters are clearly lowered. A correct half-pirouette should take three steps, and a correct whole pirouette should take five to seven steps. The canter pirouette requires the greatest collection and is a strenuous movement for the horse – so a true pirouette should not be ridden too often.

The aids for the canter pirouette are as follows. First prepare the horse with several half-halts, so that his inside hind leg is brought well under him. The horse must be kept straight in the preparation for the pirouette, then asked for inside bend in his last stride. The rider's outside lower leg should be placed behind the girth, controlling the quarters from falling out, with his inside leg encouraging the activity of the inside hind leg. The rider's weight is on the inside seat bone, and his body is very erect. The hands, although controlling the forehand bend and the direction, should be light and should allow the horse to keep the rhythm of the canter. The rider controls the steps with his inside leg and the outside rein, while maintaining the bend with the inside rein. He must keep the rhythm of the canter with the inside leg but without upsetting the balance when coming out of the pirouette.

Right canter pirouette
1 Rider sits upright.
2 Right leg on girth.
3 Left leg behind girth.
4 Right rein asks for right flexion and directs the movement.
5 Left rein controls the outside shoulder.
6 Rider looks in direction of movement.

THE AIDS FOR RIGHT CANTER PIROUETTE

- In collected canter, ask for half-halt.
- Rider sits upright in saddle.
- Right seat-bone forward.
- Right leg on girth for horse to bend around, and to keep inside hind leg active.
- Left leg behind girth.
- Right rein asks for flexion and directs the movement.
- Left rein controls the outside shoulder.
- Rider looks in direction of movement.

Exercises for canter half-pirouette

This exercise makes full use of the manège. Canter down the long side; just before the corner, collect the canter, ask for a half-halt, and do a half-pirouette. Continue on the diagonal and ask for another half-pirouette at the point marked.

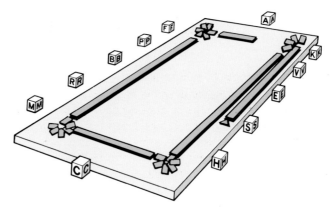

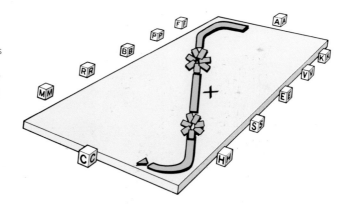

Exercises for canter pirouette

Canter down the long side of the arena, towards the end, collect the canter, ask for a half-halt, then do a half-pirouette. Continue on down quarter line of arena, then, before the corner, do a three-quarter pirouette. Proceed across the short side, do another three-quarter pirouette, and so on. Finish by riding a half-pirouette or a flying change.

Exercises for 360° canter pirouettes

1 In collected canter, turn across the diagonal of the manège and ask for a 360° pirouette. Canter for a few strides, ask for a flying change, then do another 360° pirouette before rejoining the track just before the corner.

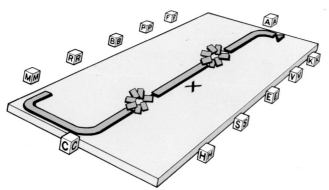

2 This is the same exercise, done down the centre line of the manège. These exercises are both good training for tests.

103

1

2

360° Pirouette in canter
In the sequence of pictures on these and the following two pages, a 360° pirouette in canter is being performed. In the first illustration *(above)*, a half-halt has been asked for, the horse has responded, and his ears show that he is listening for the rider's next instruction. The rider then places her left leg well behind the girth and asks for the inside bend with the right rein, and by placing her right leg on the girth. The horse steadies himself in response, and takes the first steps of the pirouette. By the final picture on the opposite page, he has completed about one-third of the turn.

5

3

4

6

7

8

9

12

13

360° Pirouette in canter (continued)

In these pictures, the horse continues to come steadily further round to complete the full pirouette. Throughout the movement, the rider maintains the steady rhythm, keeping her legs in canter position – the inside leg maintains the 'jump' in canter, whilst the outside leg controls the quarters. As the pirouette nears completion, the rider prepares to ride forward, using the inside leg. In the final picture of the sequence, the horse is moving quietly forward in collected canter.

10

11

14

15

CHAPTER SEVEN

ADVANCED DRESSAGE

THE CHALLENGE OF
ADVANCED MOVEMENTS

THE ZIGZAG IN CANTER

FLYING CHANGES IN SEQUENCE

THE PIAFFE

PASSAGE

Dutch Courage, ridden in the beautiful setting of Goodwood Park. He is performing passage, which is one of the most dramatic of the advanced dressage movements.

THE ADVANCED MOVEMENTS

Advanced dressage is the most exciting and rewarding part of riding and training. It is only when all the elementary and early training has been mastered that the horse can be ridden in to these advanced movements. As always, the rider has to be a dispassionate critic both with himself and his horse.

The horse's paces must be regular and free, with a balanced movement which appears light and easy for the horse to perform. His hindquarters should be engaged and full of impulsion. He should be soft in his back, neck and lower jaw, accepting the guidance and balancing effect of the rider's legs, seat and hands. These aids should now be so subtle and refined that the horse seems to be performing all the movements on his own. The impulsion, activity and suppleness of the joints must be free from resistance. When the horse is responding to the aids calmly and without hesitation, he performs the movements required with precision and in both mental and physical balance.

THE CHALLENGE TO HORSE AND RIDER

A horse that has been correctly and fairly trained will find dressage a challenge and he will enjoy pleasing his rider. Just as a horse enjoys jumping if he has been properly introduced to the jump, and if he receives praise for his efforts, the equivalent is true of the dressage horse, the cutting horse, the driving horse, and so on. However, the horse that is not well taught or sensibly handled for his particular temperament will rush his jump or get over-excited and tense because he cannot understand what is being asked of him. Such tension may also derive from the rider's own behaviour if he seems never satisfied or over-demanding. The horse perhaps feels that he did what the aids asked him but, without praise or recognition of his efforts, he becomes confused, tense and unhappy.

Self-criticism and taking the time to study your training is very important. No one is perfect, and there is surely no rider who has not regretted some hasty action or lapse of understanding when training or riding. When something is wrong, the horse is the first to tell you by his reactions, and you have then to set about repairing the damage and misunderstanding. If, for instance, the horse has made several mistakes when asked for flying changes, you may have then over-reacted with your aids, becoming a little rough and confusing the horse, and so still not achieving a correct change. It is evident that something is wrong and

you must stop, study the situation – particularly yourself – and go back to perfecting the balance and collection, the softness and swing. At this stage, do not ask for a flying change at all. Leave the changes for perhaps several days and work on transitions to simple change and lateral work to help perfect the collection. When you have really regained control of the horse's balance and yourself, ask for the flying change again but, even now, ask only for very few and be satisfied with small, gradual improvements.

Awareness of your problems is far more important than the problems themselves. Common sense and the rider's feel and understanding of his mount are vital. The horse is a living, moving, sensitive animal and just as easily distracted as a young child is from his work. When riding dressage you must capture his attention and perfect your own powers of concentration too. The horse can do only what is asked of him, and his balance, attention and paces are performed at their best only when the rider is in full control of his seat, legs and hands and moves in complete harmony with the horse's own movements.

Christopher Bartle and Wily Trout, competing at the Goodwood International Dressage Competitions, 1980. He is demonstrating the correct riding position, going forward in medium trot. The horse is showing a good outline, with strong activity coming from the hind legs.

THE ZIGZAG IN CANTER

Having perfected the lateral movements and single flying changes, the zigzag in canter can be practised. The zigzag in collected canter is usually ridden on the centre line with four steps in half-pass one way, a flying change, and eight steps the other way, then another eight steps in half-pass, followed by another flying change, and then four steps back to the centre line. The steps should be evenly distributed either side of the centre line, with the flying changes performed on the fourth stride and the eighth stride. When the horse is about to make the third and seventh step sideways in half-pass, the rider uses a little more outside leg to bring the horse's quarters over so that they are straight behind the forelegs before the flying change is performed.

When practising this movement, the horse must be really obedient, and to help balance him the rider should ask for small half-halts whenever necessary. It is often helpful, too, to alter the number of steps. Ten or twelve steps may be better for a young horse who perhaps needs more time to establish his balance in the half-pass. Another useful preparation is to take the horse into a large field, ride straight towards some object as a marker for yourself, then practise the zigzag and change until you really get the feel for the movement. If you can persuade someone to mow the grass like a centre line, this is even better and helps you regulate the steps of the half-pass so that they are really evenly distributed.

In the Grand Prix test, the zigzag has three and six steps and more changes of direction and, when perfected, the movement should look smooth and well balanced.

Zigzag in canter
1 Right leg on girth for horse to bend around.
2 Left leg behind girth to maintain new right canter half-pass.
3 Right rein asks for right bend.
4 Left rein controls horse's shoulders.
5 Rider looks in direction of movement.
6 Horse is in second step of right canter.

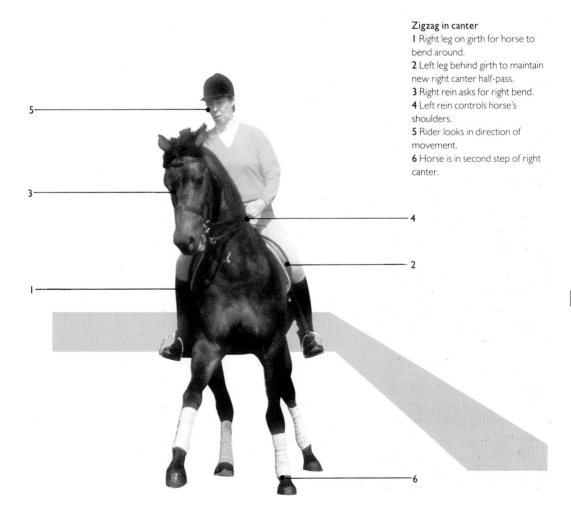

Zigzag in canter
1 Coming out of the corner in collected canter, the rider asks for the right bend and immediately gives the aids for right half-pass.

2 The horse is still in right half-pass – he should maintain this for six or eight steps.

3 Now he is performing the flying change to the left, responding to the rider's change of aids – her left leg is on the girth, her right leg behind the girth; the left rein is indicating left flexion, the right rein is controlling the shoulders, and she is looking in the new direction.

4 This is the last stride of the half-pass left. The rider is in the process of changing the aids again, pushing the horse's quarters well over towards the track before asking for the flying change.

5 The horse has just finished the right flying change; note the slight tilting of his head during the change of bend.

6 The new half-pass is well established, the horse stepping forwards and sideways with the right flexion.

Exercises for zigzag half-pass

In collected canter, turn down the centre of the manège, and half-pass left for three or four steps. Ask for flying change and then half-pass right for six to eight strides. Ask for flying change, and half-pass left for the same number of steps. Continue down manège in this way.

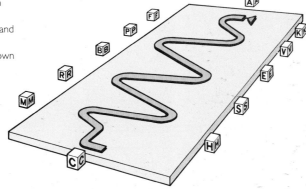

FLYING CHANGES IN SEQUENCE, OR TEMPO CHANGES

These are really fascinating movements, and a great challenge to the rider, for without feel and timing they cannot be performed correctly. First, you must have the single flying changes really strongly established (see Chapter 6, p. 96). The rider must make sure he is sitting correctly and securely, without shifting his weight. The aids must be firm, so that the horse knows what is being asked of him.

The practice of riding around the manège, changing to counter-canter can be used. The rider first changes two or three times on the long side. If the horse remains in balance after each change, then a change can be made every sixth or fifth stride. It is important that the rider learns to count the strides in the early stages of tempo changes because it becomes more difficult as they get quicker. One way of counting I have found helpful is 1 2 3 2 2 3 3 2 3 4 2 3 5, or 1 2 2 2 3 2 4 2 5 2 6 2 7. This way you always know exactly how many changes you have made.

PROBLEMS IN CHANGES OF TEMPO

When performing tempo changes, as I have said previously, the role of the rider is crucial. He must make sure he asks the horse for the change at the correct moment of the preceding stride.

Only a few changes should be ridden to start, then the horse should be allowed to walk and rewarded with a stroke on the neck. If he becomes over-excited when

1

2

3

4

asked to change, just do two steps, then halt and praise. After a time, the horse will anticipate the halt and praise and begin to relax. At this point, he can perform a further, less excited change, which is then also rewarded. Often with an excitable horse it is important to keep his concentration by giving him variety – going from changes to a half-pass or working on a circle, then a few more tempo changes.

If the horse always does five time changes when the rider thinks he has asked only for four, then the aids are being applied too late. Often in this case a slight half-halt in the preceding stride is helpful. Another problem is when the horse throws in a change without being asked. In this case, the rider must keep the lower leg more firmly round the horse in the canter position he wishes to stay in. A quite different fault is the canter slowing down and losing impulsion. In this case, the horse must be ridden with strong forward-driving seat aids with perhaps a few

tempo changes, then a medium canter, and so on until he gains the necessary impulsion.

The tempo changes must be practised on the diagonal, because a horse is sometimes a bit lost without the support of a wall. Later, when the changes are established

THE AIDS FOR FLYING CHANGES IN SEQUENCE

- For one-time changes, keep both legs against the horse's sides. As change from one step to another is made, automatically apply and release leg pressure.
- For two-, three-, or four-time changes, hold horse in canter until new change is wanted, then actively apply leg aids.

5

6

7

One-time flying changes
1 The rider first asks for a half-halt, which the horse is performing here.
2 Now the rider has asked with her right leg for the horse to change to a left lead.
3 The horse has changed to the left. So now a passive right leg from the rider allows him to change back to the right.
4 As the horse places his right hind leg on the ground, the rider allows her left leg to become passive and uses her right leg behind the girth.

5 The rider's right leg is moved forward to become more passive. The left leg will be moved back to ask for the change.
6 The horse is already changing on to the right leg, so, again, the rider is looking towards the left change.
7 The right leg is brought on to the girth, and the left leg taken behind the girth to maintain right canter.

in four-time, three-time and two-time, is the moment to go into the field and ride them down the mown centre line to help you keep the horse straight and in the correct rhythm. A useful exercise is to ride an advanced horse in four-time, three-time and two-time, and then work back up to four-time again. This helps to keep the freedom and swing of the canter and checks that your horse is obedient and calm. Of course, the rider will have many occasions when the horse falls on to the hand, gains too much speed, and so on. In these cases, a few half-halts will set his balance in a position off his forehand, and he will then be able to relax into the movement.

FLYING CHANGES ON EVERY STRIDE

When asking for the flying change at every stride, the horse must be very well balanced, with a light forehand to give him the freedom to skip from step to step. The aids for the rider begin with half-halt. Start to ask for the change with the outside leg, almost immediately stroking the horse with the other leg and keeping both legs close to his side. Then, as his body naturally curves a little as each hind leg swings forward under his belly, so he gives himself the aid for the next change. When you want to stop, place your legs in the position for canter right or left

Exercises for sequence flying changes
1 Here the rider asks for four-time flying changes on the diagonal – that is, cantering three strides, then doing a flying change, cantering three more strides, and so on. Start in left canter just

before the corner, then leave the track, flying change right, left, right, left, and rejoin the track.

2 Turn down the arena just in from the track to do these three-time changes. This is a good training movement – it ensures that the horse is going straight without 'leaning' on the wall for guidance.

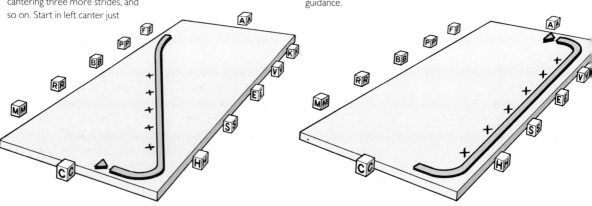

3 Canter right-handed, then ride across the diagonal doing two-time changes, rejoining the track cantering in the opposite direction. Alternatively, try doing two-time changes in a half-circle, as illustrated at bottom of diagram.

4 One-time changes on the diagonal, or on a half-circle. Flying changes are easiest to perform on the straight – either on the diagonal or just off the track. The wall of the arena can impede the movement. Doing them in a circle is a particularly good test of

balance and obedience. In a large arena, try doing them in a serpentine too. The more difficult the movement, the more marks you get in an advanced freestyle dressage test.

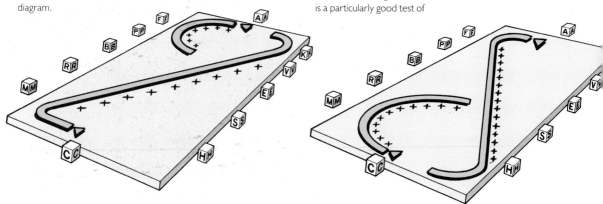

When teaching the horse to make one-tempo changes, be content with very small beginnings. First ask for just two successive one-tempo changes — one-two — and then continue on in canter, quietly rebalancing the horse. This sequence can then be repeated, working down the long side of the *manège*, until the horse is managing several two-step, one-time changes, at shorter intervals. Over a few weeks you can progress to making three successive one-time changes and so on, gradually building up the number of changes, until the horse is being ridden straight and quietly on the long side and across the diagonal repeating the tempo changes at decreasing and then lengthening intervals, as requested.

FAULTS IN FLYING CHANGES ON EVERY STRIDE

The most difficult fault to cure is that of a horse which changes with a high and swinging croup. This looks ugly, and tempo changes should be attempted only in very short, controlled sequences. The croup comes up because the horse has learnt that, with a big jump behind, he can loosen the rider's seat. This is an evasion and must be corrected quietly, just as it was when first teaching the single flying change.

If the horse shifts his quarters to the inside, this is because the new inside hind leg is not coming forward enough. The rider can correct this by using a slightly more forward-pushing seat in the change. Although an experienced rider should be able to accomplish this

easily, a less able rider may find it a help to place poles on the ground near the track where he is going to ask for the changes. The horse will naturally not like to touch the poles with his feet and so will remain straighter in the change. A line of poles placed across the diagonal about half a metre (18 inches) apart can make a great difference to a swinging horse. The trainer can then correct the rider's seat so that he learns to have more influence over the horse. With this fault, the rider/trainer must realize that there is a problem with the canter and so the pace has to be improved, making the horse lighter in his forehand. A number of exercises help, including forward to working canter and transitions to collection, as well as half-passes, then forward to working canter. Some steps in shoulder-in then forward to working canter bring the inside leg more forward so that the horse is better prepared for canter flying changes.

Sometimes, a young horse makes as if to change but not finish the movement. In this case, the rider should move the new inside and new outside leg a little more obviously so that the horse has more freedom to change the legs over. Sometimes it is enough to move and lighten the new inside leg only.

If the horse tends to gain speed in the one-tempo changes, then he is not in true balance. To correct this, the rider must feel for the moment when the horse is beginning to lose his balance and quietly ask for walk and give praise. If this happens several times, the horse will begin to anticipate walk and then the rider will be able to

COMMON FAULTS IN FLYING CHANGE: CAUSES AND CURES

- The horse is not obeying the right change aid he has been given, and has dropped his right hind leg instead of bringing it forward.
- He is thus cantering one stride disunited, sometimes called 'late behind'.

- To correct, bring horse back to walk and start again. This will instil into his mind the idea of collection in times of trouble.
- Riding the horse onward to get out of trouble might only encourage him to rush forward.

use his seat aids to help balance the horse through a longer sequence of changes. During a long line of one-tempo changes, the rider needs to give some small half-halts to keep the horse in balance. Eventually, however, a very advanced and well-trained horse will find one-time changes as easy as a child finds skipping down the road. When the rider feels he has the canter balance to perfection, then changes can be performed all round the *manège* and on circles.

THE PIAFFE

The piaffe is a movement requiring the ultimate in trot collection. It is a two-time pace which needs plenty of impulsion. The hind legs are brought well under the horse thus lightening the forehand, the croup is lowered, the legs are lifted in a springy cadenced trot, and the horse remains on the spot throughout. The knee, hock and fetlock joints should be flexed so that the toe of the foreleg is above the fetlock joint of the opposite leg. The hind feet should be raised and flexed so that the toe is at fetlock height. Horses with naturally round action usually perform piaffe with higher steps than a flatter-moving horse. However, the cadence, power and correct outline

The piaffe
This piaffe is slightly lacking in impulsion from behind, and the forelegs are too far underneath the horse.
1 Rider's seat is light, gently riding the horse forward.
2 Legs swinging in rhythm with the steps required.
3 Hands lightly controlling the impulsion created by the seat and legs.

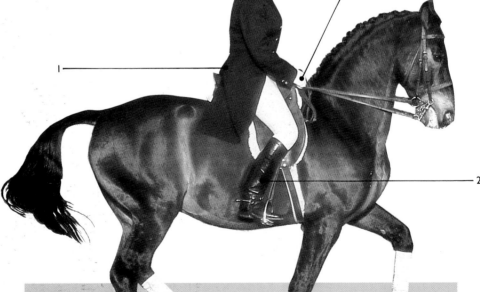

is more important than the height of the steps.

THE AIDS

The aids for piaffe begin with half-halt, then ride forward with your seat aids while remaining light so that the horse can raise his back and lower his croup. The lower leg aids are very soft and used in rhythm with the steps. Some horses take up the steps more readily with alternate leg aids, whereas others are happier when both legs are used together. The hands are very light and just indicate that the movement is practically stationary while retaining a feeling of forwardness. In an experienced partnership, the rider can usually initiate piaffe just by sitting in an erect manner, lightly touching the horse with the legs and holding him stationary with the erectness of his upper

THE AIDS FOR PIAFFE

- Ask for a half-halt.
- Ride horse forward lightly with an upright seat and very light, soft rein aids.
- Leg aids should be soft and swinging.
- Rider should take cue from the horse – if he is stepping well, diagonal leg aids should be applied lightly.
- If horse is 'sticking', apply both legs together in rhythm with the horse's steps to initiate forward movement and create more impulsion, but not to quicken the steps.

A classical piaffe
The corrective aids shown have made this piaffe very springy, energetic and classical.
1 Rider's seat is used a little more strongly to ride forward and create extra energy.
2 Diaphragm is held a little more erect to lighten the forehand.
3 Legs used together to create more activity.
4 Hands are very soft to allow the energy and to help give spring to the movement.
5 Rider is looking up and ahead.

CORRECTING FAULTS IN PIAFFE

1

2

3

4

5

1 The forelegs are too far back and under the horse, so that the hind and forelegs are too close together. The horse has dropped slightly behind the rider and is tending to be overbent and tense in his back.

2 and **3** The rider is using a little more seat and leg aid to push the horse into a more forward contact.

4 The horse has raised his shoulders; the forelegs have therefore moved forward and are not so far underneath his belly.

5 The fore and hind legs are now in a good position, not nearly as close together as in 1. The steps and outline are greatly improved.

body. The rein aids keep the horse lightly on the bit. The piaffe is usually shown on a straight line for 12 to 15 steps, or can be performed in a pirouette.

TEACHING PIAFFE IN HAND

To teach your horse piaffe takes time and patience. There are two ways — in hand, and with the rider. To work the horse in hand, he should have a snaffle bridle, roller, side reins and a cavesson fitted. With large horses, an assistant may be needed to take the rein from the centre of the cavesson ring and stand on the near side, close to the horse's head. The trainer, standing near the hindquarters on the near side, takes a lunge rein which is attached to the off-side ring of the cavesson and comes over the horse's back. A schooling whip with a short free end is used to touch the hind legs of the horse.

To start, the side reins are attached to the snaffle bit, the horse standing on the track. The trainer taps the near hind leg with the whip until the horse raises his leg, receiving praise for his efforts. The process is repeated to the off hind until the horse realizes that the tap with the whip means he must raise the leg. The assistant at this time should be facing the horse's tail and keeping control of the horse with his left hand on the lead rein. When the horse has lifted both legs a few times, the assistant should turn, walk him forward and halt again. The assistant turns to face the hindquarters again, while the trainer asks the horse to raise the hind legs.

High-couraged horses usually react quickly to the touch with the whip, and a trainer has to be very careful not to use it too strongly with them. However, a heavier horse may need quite a sharp tap. Plenty of praise when the horse shows a good, quick lift of the hind leg soon teaches him what is required. After a few short sessions of no longer than four or five minutes a day, you can try asking for some piaffe-like steps. A stationary piaffe must never be attempted until the horse is advanced in this movement, so first move the horse forward with some short trot steps. With a very sensitive horse it is sometimes even better to start in walk. A couple of touches with the whip and at the same time a click with the tongue will cause him to make a few little trot steps which should be immediately rewarded with a halt and a stroke on the neck or a titbit. Gradually over several days the horse will come to understand what is required of him.

The assistant faces backwards when asking for piaffe, and forwards when relaxing and giving praise or walking. Later, the trainer takes up the assistant's position and can then work the horse by himself with the whip in his right hand when facing backwards and the cavesson rein in his left hand. The horse soon associates the trainer's turn and his voice with impulsion and piaffe steps. The whip may be dispensed with as soon as the horse understands. However, you must have a whip when training, so that any fault or hanging back can be corrected. Where you touch the horse on the legs very much depends what sort of reaction he has to the whip. It may be best in front of the cannon bone or, alternatively, at the back of the leg below the hock. Care must be taken if the whip is ever used above the hock because this can teach the horse to bring his hind legs up and out behind, rather than coming under the body. Using the whip on the croup as seen in some books is apt to make the horse bring his croup high. This can be a help, though, for a horse whose hind legs come too much under the body.

Teaching Piaffe in hand

The horse is tacked up, with a roller and side-reins, a snaffle bridle and a cavesson. The assistant stands facing the horse's head with a lunge rein. The trainer holds the offside lunge rein, which is brought over the horse's back, in her left hand, and has a whip in her right hand. The horse is making good piaffe steps, so there is no need to touch him with the whip. After a few steps, he will be halted and praised. In the early stages, it is very important that he is made to go forward in the piaffe steps; only a trained horse would be expected to piaffe nearly on the spot, as seen here.

COLLECTION AND ELEVATION

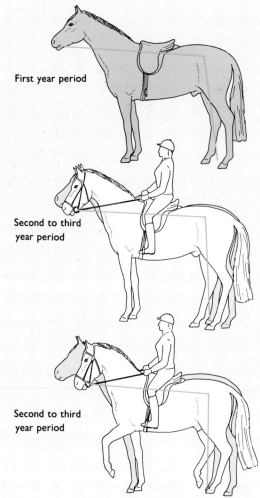

First year period

Second to third year period

Second to third year period

Third year period

Collection and elevation
Diagram to show how a horse progresses towards collection and elevation during dressage training. In the first diagram, training has scarcely begun – the angle taken from the point of the horse's nose to his hindquarters and down to his hind feet is correspondingly wide. As training progesses, the horse's outline is shortened and becomes more pronounced, and his head and neck carriage more elevated. Finally, as he becomes sufficiently supple and well trained to perform the advanced movements of piaffe and passage, you can see how the angle from nose to hindquarters to foot has become considerably more acute. Training to this stage takes some years and cannot be rushed. It is important that the horse is well balanced at every stage of the training; otherwise it will be impossible for him to progress towards ultimate collection and elevation.

Quiet work teaching the horse piaffe in hand will really make him engage his hind legs. However, these must be short lessons. Many horses are spoilt and upset by people asking too much from them and tiring their muscles.

When the horse is working fluently with piaffe in hand, a rider can be put on the horse and some forward steps asked of him with the trainer guiding from the ground. Gradually the rider gives the aids for piaffe, still using the voice and the whip, if necessary in this transition period. As the partnership progresses, the trainer can be dispensed with, and the rider takes up control.

TEACHING PIAFFE WITH THE RIDER

When teaching the horse from the beginning with the rider, it is important to use to your advantage the natural energy and impulsion created by circumstances such as turning for home when out hacking, or opening the door of the indoor school. As the horse offers piaffe, be quick to recognize this and give him an aid for what he is doing, and lots of praise for good, springy steps. Over a time, you can teach a horse piaffe this way. Another method is to shorten the trot steps with short half-halts and ask for piaffe. Then praise and trot on again. If you clearly give the same aids in the same place often enough over a period of time, the horse will come to understand what is required of him.

When teaching piaffe, it is usually easier to start the training when the horse is fresh. As the horse progresses and performs the forward piaffe steps with ease, the rider should shorten the steps very gradually with one to three steps more on the spot. It is the steps which are shortened, never the reins. Strong tension on the rein will soon put the horse's weight on his shoulders and destroy the action of the forelegs. The horse must be on the bit. Any tendency to come up with the head and neck will hollow his back and his hind legs will not be engaged. If this happens, the rider must take the horse forward in trot and push him into a very rounded outline until his energy is coming strongly into the hand. The piaffe steps can then be asked for again and the rein lightened a little. If there is a tendency for the horse to come above the bit, ride him more forward into the hand again or take him into a volte and then try again.

The art of training a horse for piaffe is to make him really enjoy pleasing the rider. A classical piaffe is asked for with very light aids – a piaffe demanded with the spur is never attractive for the spectator or the horse.

PASSAGE

This is a movement which both looks and feels very dramatic. The horse springs forward in a very slow cadenced trot, the moment of suspension increased by high, prolonged steps. The feet are at about the same level as in the piaffe but the horse is not so rounded in the croup. The beauty of the movement comes from the impulsion and contained energy.

The passage and piaffe movements, and the transitions from one to the other, are the ultimate in collection, submission and obedience. The rhythm from piaffe to passage should remain steady and consistent throughout the transition, although this is difficult to achieve. There are few horses who have the natural ability to perform these two movements classically but, with correct training, many horses could put up a good show.

THE AIDS

The aids for passage comprise riding with the seat forward but light, both legs behind the girth asking for the rhythm, and the hands distributing the energy. The legs are held round the horse and used to indicate an upward lift with each step.

THE AIDS FOR PASSAGE
■ From walk, trot or piaffe, ask for half-halt.
■ Lighten seat.
■ Close both legs round horse.
■ Ride horse forward, using seat and leg aids in rhythm with the steps of the passage.
■ Hands lightly control the balance and speed of the pace, and the rhythm of the steps.

Riding passage
1 Rider's seat is light, but gently driving the horse into forward movement.
2 Both legs are closed around the horse, nudging his sides in rhythm with the steps.
3 Hands are held lightly to control the horse's energy and direction.
4 Diaphragm is held erect.

TEACHING PASSAGE

There are several ways to teach passage. It is usually easier than teaching the piaffe because it is forward-moving, and can be developed from it by riding out of the piaffe with forward-driving aids into an allowing but regulating hand. The collected trot can be used and, with several half-halts in the rhythm required, the horse can be put into the passage. Alternatively, ride forward into a strong but slow medium trot; then, with half-halts again in rhythm, bring the impulsion into passage steps. The rider must be careful to keep the horse round and on the bit. When both passage and piaffe are established, the transitions between the two can be practised.

It is usually better to teach the piaffe first. If horses learn the passage first, they often find it difficult to achieve a piaffe of the same calibre as those who have really learned to sit and work with energy from the hind legs. Horses trained in passage first, usually make the piaffe look extremely laboured for both horse and rider. There are of course a few exceptions to the rule, in this as in every aspect of dressage. Dressage is such a close partnership between horse and rider that every horse calls forth a different response from the rider. Of course, this is part of the secret of dressage and the reason why, after 30 years of working with horses, I am still as fascinated by it as ever.

Riding piaffe into passage
1 Here the horse is in **piaffe**. The rider places both legs just behind the girth and rides the horse forward with her seat. By closing her legs steadily round the horse, she moves him forward into **passage**.

2 Here the horse has achieved passage. He is now powerfully pushing forward, with elevated, springing steps.

3 The passage is now being maintained with leg, seat and rein aids. The horse is showing big, swinging passage steps.

COMPETING IN DRESSAGE

TESTS: THE SIX STANDARDS

BITS AND BRIDLES

THE REQUIRED DRESS

THE RULES

RIDING IN

Dressage competitions are not only for the experts; there are classes for all standards – from novice to advanced. Gaining experience by competing at these different levels is important for both horses and riders. Remember, a neat, smart turn-out is essential for all competitive riding, but is particularly important for the 'showy' sport of dressage.

TESTS — THE SIX STANDARDS

Dressage is an exacting and challenging sport, requiring a good deal of commitment and perseverance. Dressage competitions are a test of your skills as both rider and trainer, and in order to succeed you will need to become a shrewd critic of your own and your horse's abilities. Competitions test your ability to control your horse and to ride the required movements with precision. To do this well, you must learn to judge your horse's temperament and his understanding, so that you can guide him through the necessary steps and sequences.

In Great Britain, dressage tests are drawn up into six different standards — Preliminary, Novice, Elementary, Medium, Advanced Medium and Advanced.

PRELIMINARY

In the preliminary stages of training, dressage can be ridden at Unaffiliated competitions. This means that you do not have to register your horse with the British Horse Society Dressage Group. These competitions give you the opportunity to get your horse acquainted with the sights and sounds of other horses, and to introduce him to different arenas.

Riding and training at Preliminary level is designed to show that the horse has true natural paces; he is obedient, calm and relaxed; he is straight when ridden on straight lines, and bends when moving on curved lines; he accepts the bit; and he has balance and rhythm. He should move freely forward without collection but with active hindquarters. The test must be ridden in a snaffle bridle and all transitions may be progressive. This test demonstrates that horse and rider are beginning their training on the correct lines, and that a harmonious partnership is being established.

NOVICE

The Novice standard is a little more demanding than the Preliminary. The horse should have an improved natural outline, accept the bit willingly without tension or resistance and have a good balance and rhythm. The tests require the horse to be in self-carriage so that the rider can give and retake the reins; show some lengthened strides in trot and canter; perform some 15-metre (16-yard) circles in trot and 20-metre (22-yard) circles in canter; and show the beginnings of counter-canter and rein-back. The horse must be ridden in a snaffle bridle and transitions may be progressive. All trot work can be ridden in rising or sitting trot.

ELEMENTARY

The Elementary standard shows that the horse has progressed from the Novice standard, and that his muscular development has improved. He is more supple and round in his outline and can produce the beginning of collection. The tests demand 10-metre (11-yard) circles in

The first movement in every test is always the most difficult one! Spend time practising **a good halt** – the horse must learn to stand still obediently, placing his weight correctly on all four legs and ready to move at the rider's command.

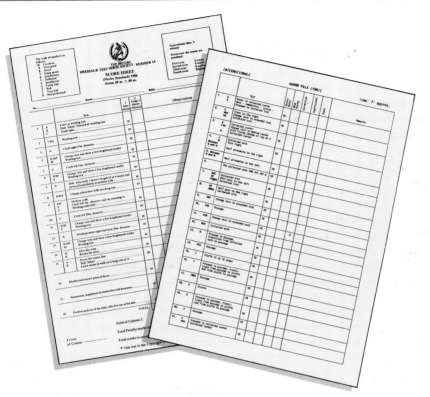

Score sheets for dressage tests at Novice and Grand Prix standards. Marks on a scale of 0-10 are allotted to each of the movements required.

trot and 15-metre (16-yard) circles in canter; counter-canter; medium, collected and working trot; shoulder-in; medium, working and collected canter; and simple changes. These tests may be ridden in a snaffle or double bridle. All trot work from Elementary standard and upwards must be executed in sitting trot.

MEDIUM

At Medium standard, the horse must be able to execute the movements required without tension and with the necessary suppleness and impulsion. He should show improved natural paces and outline, and perform the direct transitions smoothly and with precision. The tests demand working, collected, medium and extended trot; collected, medium and extended walk; working, collected, medium and extended canter; walking half-pirouettes; rein-back; shoulder-in; half-pass in trot and canter; simple change; counter-canter serpentine. The test may be ridden in a snaffle or double bridle.

ADVANCED MEDIUM

The Advanced Medium standard requires a greater degree of collection to be shown at all paces. The horse should also show more cadence and lightness in his paces. The only new movement called for is the execution of the single flying change.

ADVANCED

The horse is now required to be in perfect balance and harmony with the rider. He should be able to perform all the movements and paces of the Advanced Medium standard but with a higher degree of collection. The added movements are half and whole pirouettes in canter; counter-canter change of hand in trot and canter; flying changes in sequence at every fourth stride for riders who have just reached this standard, progressing to every stride for more experienced combinations; rein-back Schaukel; canter zigzag; piaffe and passage.

THE SCORING SYSTEM

To ride in Affiliated Dressage Competitions in Britain, you have to become a member of the BHS Dressage Group. Your horse must be registered and, if he is placed in a test, he will gain points depending on his position, as shown in the table. First place gains seven points; second place six points; and so on down to seventh position. When the horse has won fifty points, he is graded Elementary, and can no longer compete in Novice classes. Gradually, as the horse progresses in his training, he will climb up the grading ladder.

BITS AND BRIDLES

There are various snaffle bits which are permitted for dressage. The snaffle bits shown here are all allowed in competition. However, there are other snaffle bits which are not. The bit mouthpiece must be smooth with not more than two joints. There are also rubber-covered bits which are allowed, but you should never use a rubber-covered bit with a double bridle. When using the snaffle, the lightweight loose-ring bit is the kindest and most useful. Any heavy bit is apt to cause tongue problems, because a horse often finds it too heavy to carry in the mouth comfortably. Some horses prefer the double-jointed mouthpiece rather than the nutcracker action of the single joint. All bits are designed for a specific purpose, and, of course, may suit particular horses at particular times.

TYPES OF NOSEBAND

The noseband to use on a snaffle bridle should again be the one that suits your particular horse. **The Cavesson Noseband** is the one I start with for a young horse. It is free of the bit and you really feel how the horse is reacting in his lower jaw.

The Flash Noseband is a combination of both cavesson and drop noseband. It is especially useful in the way it helps to keep the bit very stable in the horse's mouth.

The Drop Noseband is perhaps the most severe, and care must be taken to make sure it is fitted correctly, as shown in Fig. 00. It must not be fitted too low on the nasal bone or adjusted too tightly. If the front part of the noseband is too long it will interfere with the bit and cause the bit to inflict constant pressure, which could cause tongue evasions.

THE DOUBLE BRIDLE

This consists of the snaffle (bridoon) and a curb or weymouth used with a curb chain. The double bridle shown here has a loose-ring bridoon and a high-ported thick mouth curb. There are many combinations from

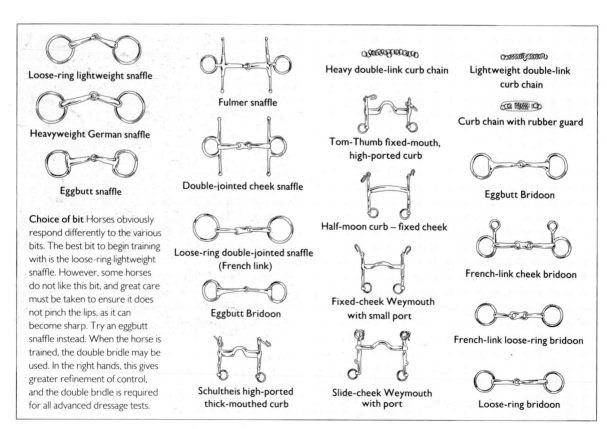

Loose-ring lightweight snaffle

Heavyweight German snaffle

Eggbutt snaffle

Choice of bit Horses obviously respond differently to the various bits. The best bit to begin training with is the loose-ring lightweight snaffle. However, some horses do not like this bit, and great care must be taken to ensure it does not pinch the lips, as it can become sharp. Try an eggbutt snaffle instead. When the horse is trained, the double bridle may be used. In the right hands, this gives greater refinement of control, and the double bridle is required for all advanced dressage tests.

Fulmer snaffle

Double-jointed cheek snaffle

Loose-ring double-jointed snaffle (French link)

Eggbutt Bridoon

Schultheis high-ported thick-mouthed curb

Heavy double-link curb chain

Tom-Thumb fixed-mouth, high-ported curb

Half-moon curb – fixed cheek

Fixed-cheek Weymouth with small port

Slide-cheek Weymouth with port

Lightweight double-link curb chain

Curb chain with rubber guard

Eggbutt Bridoon

French-link cheek bridoon

French-link loose-ring bridoon

Loose-ring bridoon

Loose-ring snaffle with drop noseband
The noseband is sitting well up on the nasal bone, the bottom line of the noseband coming just above the top of the lips. The front of the noseband must be short enough to ensure it does not press against the bit when it is done up. The back strap does up below the bit.

Double bridle
A loose-ring bridoon, used in conjunction with a Schultheis fixed-mouth curb and a correctly fitted curb chain. Note how the angle of this is approximately 45° to the horse's lips.

which to choose. Some horses prefer a certain amount of tongue pressure and these require a bit with a very small port. Others require plenty of tongue room with no pressure on the tongue. A horse with a dry mouth may prefer a mouthpiece which moves as he uses his tongue.

In all cases, the curb chain must be correctly fitted. It should be turned in a clockwise direction until completely flat. It should be adjusted so that the cheek does not come back more than 45° from the line of the horse's lips. The chain may be covered with rubber or leather.

THE DRESSAGE SADDLE

The saddle is designed to provide the closest contact between the rider's legs and the horse. The most important consideration is that the saddle should fit the rider. It should have a narrow waist, and the flaps should be quite long, to fit the leg of the rider and give a little support. Some riders like to have straps attached to the flaps to prevent them from moving. Saddles should have a good, uniform fit over the horse's back and distribute the rider's weight evenly. The knee roll is there to suit the rider and can be altered. The girth is either attached under the saddle flap, or a Lonsdale girth can be used.

Dressage saddles
There are many different types made nowadays. On the left is a Stubben-Tristan – a useful saddle which fits most horses well. On the right is a British-made Lux saddle, made specifically for a horse and rider. It has a good, comfortable seat and, as in most dressage saddles, a straight cut flap.

THE REQUIRED DRESS

NOVICES AND ELEMENTARY TESTS

The dress required for riding Novice and Elementary tests is a tweed coat, buff breeches, coloured stock or collar and tie, light-coloured gloves, black or brown boots, and a jockey cap or bowler.

MEDIUM TO ADVANCED TESTS

At this level, it is correct to wear a dark navy or black coat, light-coloured or white breeches, white gloves, a white or cream stock or collar and tie, black boots and a jockey cap or bowler. Spurs are compulsory from Medium standard upwards, and should be correctly fitted with the shank pointing downwards and the side of the spur lying on the seam of the boot.

ADVANCED TESTS

It is now correct to wear a dark navy or black tail-coat, white or cream stock, white gloves, white breeches, black boots, spurs and a top hat. When ladies are wearing a bowler or top hat, the hair must be neatly put up so that it fits close to the brim of the hat and is not bouncing around on the coat collar. The brim of the hat should be level with the ground when the rider's head is in the correct position. It should be placed just above the eyebrows and not sit on the back of the head. A hairnet should always be worn when riding. Jewellery is inappropriate and can be very dangerous. Make-up should be used discreetly and in moderation.

It is compulsory to wear a riding hat at all times when mounted at a dressage competition, and the rider should always give the appearance of being neat and tidy for this very exacting sport.

(*Far left*) Rider and horse correctly turned out for a **novice dressage competition**. The horse is in a snaffle bridle with a flash noseband. The rider is wearing fawn breeches, a tweed coat, light-coloured gloves, and a collar and tie. Her hair is held neatly in a hairnet. Whip and spurs are permissible in novice competitions.

(*Left*) Here the rider is dressed for a **medium competition**. She is wearing a dark coat, light breeches, gloves and a white stock. Spurs are compulsory at this level, and a whip is permissible.

Dress for **advanced competition**. The rider is wearing a tail-coat, top hat, white breeches, gloves and stock. The hair is neatly put up close to the brim of the hat, and make-up should be worn in moderation. Spurs are compulsory – and so is a double bridle for the horse. Whips are allowed in national competitions, except for championships and selection trials. They are also not allowed in international competitions.

TURN-OUT FOR THE DRESSAGE HORSE: PLAITING

The horse should look as well turned out as his rider. His mane should be plaited and he should be well groomed with oiled hoofs. Horses who have a full tail should have them plaited. Plaiting is an art which some people find extremely difficult. There are two ways of plaiting: the English and the Continental.

THE ENGLISH PLAIT

This is worked with a needle and thread. The mane must be the correct length, about 15 centimetres (six inches) long. Measure out about 76 mm (three inches) width of hair with a mane comb, dampen the mane and start to plait the hair, keeping the plait tight and firm. When you get almost to the bottom, turn the plait up and hold the free end between your finger and thumb. Put the needle through the free end and take the knot up to the root; wrap some thread around the end and, holding the little hairs, put the needle through the end again. Once the plait is firm and long, turn it up twice, sewing as you go. Finish by pulling any loose ends into the plait with the thread. A well-plaited horse will have about ten to 15 plaits down his neck. All should be evenly spaced and look neat.

THE CONTINENTAL PLAIT

Start the same way as for the English plait, but finish the end of the plait with an elastic band only turning it up once, so that the plait is about 50 to 76 mm (two to three inches) long. When the mane is completely plaited up with the elastic bands, then white adhesive tape is placed over the band. You should put the tape round at least twice for security and make sure it is well stuck. You must be careful to make sure that the white tape is in the same position on each plait or it may make the neck look an odd shape.

1

2

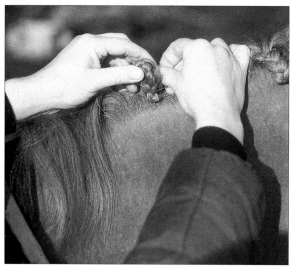

3

4

5

The Continental plait

1 The mane is first divided equally into an odd number of sections. Dampen them one at a time and plait right to the bottom of the hair.

2 Turn up the ends and secure the bottom with an elastic band, then

3, turn the plait under, securing again with the rubber band.

4 Wind white adhesive tape tightly round the top of the plait.

5 A fully plaited mane. Make sure the white tape is in the same position for each plait, otherwise the neck will look irregularly shaped.

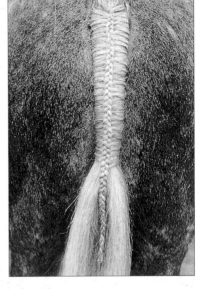

The English plait. Plaiting a horse's mane smartens his appearance and shows off the neck to advantage. Give yourself plenty of time for plaiting, but do it on the morning of the show; if left overnight, the horse is almost bound to rub the plaits.

Correctly plaited tail. It is harder to plait a tail correctly than it is a mane. Only plait the tail if you can do it well; it would be far better to have a neatly pulled and washed unplaited tail than a badly plaited one.

THE TAIL

The tail can be either pulled and banged, or plaited and banged. If plaited, it must first be well brushed out, so that there are no knots. Then take some hair from each side of the top of the tail alternately, making it into a single plait down the centre. The plaited hairs should be about half to three-quarters of the length of the tailbone. When you have finished taking in the side hairs, then plait the lower part. Turn up the end and sew it. Then, putting the needle into the base of the side plait and bringing it through to the top of the plait, sew down the side plait to the end and finish. A horse with a plaited tail should not be left in a stable without a tail bandage because he could rub the plait out.

THE *MANÈGE* OR COMPETITION ARENA

The manège is a flat measured area of grass or sand. The alternative sizes of a dressage arena are 40×20 metres (44×22 yards) or 60×20 metres (66×22 yards). The area is marked with letters which are placed at intervals outside the arena, about one metre (yard) from the sides of the track. The entrance is at 'A'. There are from one to three judges who are placed at the 'C' end of the arena. The master judge is at 'C'; the two others are placed near 'H' and 'M' facing down the long side of the arena. For major international tests, there are five judges, the two others placed at 'B' and 'E'.

RIDING THE TEST SUCCESSFULLY

Dressage tests are divided into short movements and each of these is given a mark from nought to ten. The horse gaining the highest number of points is the winner. The precise divisions of the tests are of little importance to the rider, and I explain the various movements elsewhere. It is the way the rider performs the test that is important. It is vital to carry out the required movement at the correct place and to ride on the track all the time except when otherwise instructed. Riding into the corners is very important – is the horse making a corner or a circle? The judge must be able to see the difference before he can give a mark. The circles must be round and of the correct size. All these important points come into the horse's basic training and must be thoroughly mastered.

In the early training and tests, every transition can be progressive, and so the majority of the weight of both horse and rider is naturally on the shoulders. As the horse's training progresses, so the weight is gradually transferred to the hind legs and all transitions can then be direct, because the balance is then fully under control.

THE RULES OF DRESSAGE

Dressage rules can alter from year to year, but when you become a member of the Dressage Group in Britain you are sent a rule book and a schedule of all the competitions to be held during the year. The main things to remember are:

■ The horse must wear a bit or bridle recognized in the rule book.

■ No martingales maybe used when riding-in.

■ Boots or bandages are allowed for riding-in but must be removed before entering the arena.

■ Whips may be carried in dressage classes, except at selection trials, championships and international competitions.

■ Never enter the arena until the judge has signalled his indication for you to start.

■ Always ensure you are wearing the correct dress and have the correct number for your horse.

■ Make sure your horse is eligible for the class you are entering — it is your responsibility as a rider.

It is always appreciated when the organizers and secretary of a competition are thanked for their efforts in running the event.

THE COMPETITION HORSE

It costs no more to keep and produce a good dressage horse than it does any other type of horse. However, if one is looking for the ultimate in movement and elasticity, dressage horses do cost more to buy initially although sometimes you can be very lucky and find one selling cheaply. Undoubtedly, really good paces and temperament are worth paying for, because with them you are half-way to the top with your horse's natural balance.

The horse's pedigree is another important point. Have the parents performed well? Were they good movers and did they train up to the top level or did they meet with problems? Were these caused by a rider's ignorance or were the horses given the best possible chance? If you think you can cope with a few inherited difficulties, then it is really time for you to study the art of dressage and buy your horse. There is no perfect horse nor perfect rider — but some find it easier than others!

(Left) **Christopher Bartle on Wily Trout**, performing piaffe at the Aachen Championships.

(Opposite) **Pamela Hutton on Talland Blazaway**, riding left canter. She is competing at Blenheim Palace.

RIDING-IN

However good or experienced your horse is, it is essential to warm up thoroughly before a competition. When riding-in a horse for a competition, or preparing him mentally and physically for a test, one must consider several different factors. If he is a young, excitable horse and has not been to many events before, then it is sometimes best to work him really hard the day before the competition. By the time he arrives at the show, he is already quite tired and more able to relax while he is there. At future shows he should need much less work because of those first impressions. If he still gets upset and excitable at a show, take him somewhere on his own and work him quite hard in a slow, round outline in trot and canter until he settles. Then let him walk about on a long rein to see as much of the area as possible. Never leave a young horse alone in a vehicle because he may panic. A good spell loose in the field the day before an event can often help to unwind excitable horses.

Sometimes, people like to lunge their horses before competitions. This is fine, provided the horse is under control and not unsettling other horses. At the show it is a good idea to lunge with side reins attached because an extra measure of control has a sobering effect and helps the horse's concentration.

CONSIDER HIS TEMPERAMENT

If you have a quiet, ceasy horse who has a really good temperament, then treat him very much as you do at home, although you must remember that travelling may make him a little stiff and tired. In this case, I would suggest plenty of walking on a long rein first, then trot work to loosen up his muscles. It may help to practise some of the movements required in the test, transitions and checking on the straightness. Remember the first movement is sometimes the most difficult — and that is the straight entry and halt!

With a lazy horse do not overwork either him or yourself. You will need to concentrate on impulsion-creating movements, such as riding forward into medium

(Left) **Patricia Gardiner riding Wily Imp** at Blenheim Palace. She is performing an extended trot.

trot or medium canter after any lateral work, depending on the pace in which you are riding. Make your transitions quite abrupt, and even touch him with the whip when asking for the upward transitions so that his mind is alert and active. Just before you go in to the arena, give the horse a few minutes' rest while you put on your coat and take off his boots and bandages. Allow his neck to have a good stretch downwards. Once inside the arena, while you are waiting for the judge to signal you to enter the test area and start, check that the horse is really in front of your leg by asking for some transitions to medium or extended trot. You only have a minute or two before the judge sounds the bell and you enter the arena. If you are not allowed your whip, just let it slip out of your hand or present it to your groom or the ring steward.

THE WINNING ATTITUDE

Lastly, consider your own mental state. This is very important and you must not get over-excited or tense just because you are riding in front of judges. Of course, everyone gets a bit keyed up for a big occasion, but I was taught to keep calm by taking a few deep breaths, correcting my position by sitting tall and then allowing my weight to settle downwards and relax, but still keeping a lightness in my upper body. Try to pretend you are riding at home. Forget about anyone else being there, just concentrate on what you are doing and think well ahead to give yourself and the horse time to perform the movements and transitions accurately at the markers. Always be aware of noise and outside influences, and keep your horse's concentration by a little half-halt should something distract him.

To succeed in the art of dressage, the rider must be in sympathy with his horse. He must have quick reactions, and be able to adjust to his horse's movement and mood, in order to direct the balance of the horse throughout the test. The better ridden and trained the horse, the more invisible are the rider's aids, so that in an expert combination, the horse appears to be performing the movements of his own volition, without tension or nervousness.

All these tips should help you get the best out of the horse in the arena. In the end, it is your responsibility as a rider to enhance your horse's performance.

(Left) **Christine Stuckelberger and Achat**, competing at Goodwood.

CHAPTER NINE

THE STATE OF THE SPORT

TOP INTERNATIONAL RIDERS

EARLY COMPETITIONS

YOUNG STARS OF THE FUTURE

DRESSAGE TO MUSIC

THE AIM OF DRESSAGE

The Olympics, the World and European Championships – these are
the ultimate goals of ambitious and successful dressage riders. They
may be the province of the few, but everyone can enjoy the spectacle
of these events. An understanding of the years of patient training
needed for them will help to deepen the appreciation!

TOP INTERNATIONAL RIDERS

In recent years, dressage has captured the imaginations of riders all over the world, and its popularity is increasing at a tremendous pace. Television coverage of events has played a vital role in increasing the appeal of the sport, and as a result sponsors are coming forward in greater numbers.

In the competitive field, Europe has had the most success in recent years, having practised dressage since the beginning of the century, but now many other countries – such as Japan, Australia, Mexico, Brazil, the USSR, the USA and Canada – are sending teams to compete.

Many European trainers have travelled all over the world teaching, and this has raised the standard of training and riding internationally. Interest has grown everywhere, and there is now a steady demand for high-class horses to seat the ever-increasing number of riders taking up the sport. Some of the top-class riders have also given lectures and 'clinics' in many countries, and this has done a lot to foster the growth of dressage. Their expertise and experience not only improve the horses very rapidly but enthrall spectators and riders alike.

For many years, Germany has been supreme in the dressage field. However, many other nations have been having considerable recent success – the USSR, Denmark and Switzerland have all had their stars and gold medals. Such well-known riders as Dr Reiner Klimke from Germany, Anne Grethe Jensen from Denmark, Christine Stuckelberger and Otto Hoffer from Switzerland, Anne Marie Sanders Keyzer from Holland, Margit Otto-Crépin and Dominic d'Esmé from France, Christopher Bartle and myself from Great Britain have all helped stimulate interest in dressage in their own countries. Not only do good riders give the sport a standard of excellence, their successes help to get their teams a much higher place in the final results.

In dressage you are constantly striving for perfection. Nevertheless, the perfect performance, during which you are in complete harmony with your horse for ten minutes, is unknown. Yet some of the great names have put on sparkling, accurate and harmonious displays which have been real inspirations. To achieve 60 per cent of the total

(Right) **Dominique d'Esmé riding Fresh Wind** at Goodwood. Mlle d'Esmé was an event rider before concentrating on dressage. She has been placed and won competitions at Goodwood ever since its inception, as well as causing a stir with her clever riding to modern music.

(Opposite) **Dr Reiner Klimke on Ahlerich** at Aachen. Dr Klimke was Olympic gold medallist at the 1984 Olympics in Los Angeles. Among the most successful riders Germany has ever produced, he has been riding in the German dressage teams since giving up three-day eventing, some twenty years ago.

(Opposite) **Christine Stuckelberger riding Granat** in Rotterdam. This rider caused a sensation in the dressage world by winning an Olympic gold medal and the European and World titles on this great horse. Very strong and powerful, he showed particular brilliance in passage, piaffe and half passes.

(Below) **Jan Bemelmans riding Angelino** at Goodwood, performing one-time flying changes. This high class rider has been continuously successful in dressage competitions.

points in a dressage test is satisfactory. Nowadays, the stars achieve 70 per cent or more – and we may well see this standard going even higher. Important new names will emerge in the future, but of course it does take time to train a successful combination of horse and rider to Grand Prix level.

Different countries often exhibit quite distinctive styles of training and riding, and it is fascinating to observe the various national teams in action.

THE USSR

The USSR, although it competes only at the major Western dressage championships, has a particularly interesting dressage style. Their horses are very light and elegant, and are taught the advanced movements of piaffe and passage quite early in their training. There has been considerable variation in the marking of the Soviet horses because some judges, who do not consider the horses'

weight to be sufficiently on the hind legs, mark them low. Yet other judges approve of the style and give them high scores.

The marking of the piaffe, in particular, has caused considerable controversy. Some of the Soviet horses piaffe with very slow, high steps in a very good rhythm and with excellent transitions but without changing the outline. Other nations have insisted on the horse lowering his hindquarters, and this does make the transitions considerably more difficult.

EARLY COMPETITIONS

DRESSAGE IN THE UNITED STATES

It was in 1938 that the civilian population took over the responsibility of fielding international teams from the US Cavalry. In 1959 and 1960 Jessica Newberry and Trish Galvin had the first international successes. In 1959 Jessica was the leading dressage rider in Aachen, Germany, with a second place in the Grand Prix, and winning the freestyle. Trish Galvin won the Grand Prix in Aachen in 1960. In 1964, the team of Newberry, Galvin and Karen McIntosh was placed fourth at the Tokyo Olympics.

European trainers and European-trained horses played a significant role in the success of these riders and the development of the next generation. The teachings of such masters as Gunnar Anderson, St Cyr, and Richard Watjen formed the classical roots of American dressage. New riders such as Edith Masters, John Winnett and Dorothy Markis drew on this heritage in the early 1970s. Then the sensational 1978 Olympic team Bronze Medal win for the American Dressage Team of Hilda Gurney riding Keen, Dorothy Markis on Monaco, and Edith Masters on Dahlwitz, generated a wave of enthusiasm throughout the United States, resulting in more competitors, and the emerging dream of the potential of the American-bred horse, because of Keen's success. At the World Championship at Goodwood in 1978, Bao, another American-bred horse ridden by Gwen Stockebrand, was third in the Grand Prix Musical class. She was second in the same class in 1980 in the Alternate Olympics at Goodwood.

EUROPE

In Europe, competitive dressage has been developing since the early years of this century. In 1912, it was included in the Olympic Games in Stockholm. At this

stage, it was more of an obedience test and not as we know it today, but by 1936, when the Olympic Games were in Berlin, the standard had risen dramatically to include most modern movements.

GREAT BRITAIN

Since then, Britain has been gradually venturing into the sport. In the early 1950s, dressage was hardly known in Britain, but a few notable enthusiasts emerged who really cared about the horse and horsemanship. The leading names were the late Henry Wynmalen and the late Mrs V. D. S. Williams, Mrs Lorna Johnstone and, a little later, Mrs Joan Gold. They all rode and trained their own horses with occasional help from European experts, such as the late Col. Podhajsky from the Spanish Riding School, Col. Frank from the Swiss Cavalry School, and General Linkenback from Germany.

During the 1950s, there were very few competitions in Britain: you were lucky if you could find two Grand Prix classes in a year. The first British Olympic representative was Mrs Williams who, in 1956, rode her 19-year-old gelding, Pilgrim, in the Stockholm Olympics. Although unplaced, she put up a good performance and four years later she was back with her new horse, Little Model, to win eleventh place in the Rome Olympics.

Mrs Joan Gold first won a class in Aachen in 1938, but she returned inspired twenty years later to win five classes on her beautiful Thoroughbred horse, Gay Gordon — a record which has never been equalled. Even more creditable was the fact that she overcame such heroes as Dr Josef Neckermann, Bronze Medallist in the 1960 Rome Olympics, and Liselotte Linsenhoff, Bronze Medallist in the Stockholm Olympics of 1956, who later took the Gold

Medal for Germany in the 1972 Munich Olympics. Much of Mrs Gold's training had taken place in Germany where her husband was stationed, and her knowledge, enthusiasm and authority in judging is of great value to present day riders.

In 1972, Mrs Lorna Johnstone took twelfth place in the Munich Olympics. Riding the Thoroughbred El Farruco, Mrs Johnstone, then seventy years old, put up a dashing performance which was a pleasure to watch. Her alert, free-moving horse gave all he had throughout the test and they both received a tremendous ovation at the end of the performance. This helped put British dressage and the British style of riding on the international map. Mrs Johnstone produced several great horses — mostly Thoroughbreds bought out of a sale ring — the most notable being Rosie Dream, Silver Dream, Scarlet Seal, El Guapo and El Farruco. Lorna was highly respected by all riders and the fact that she hunted most of her horses all winter as well is a testament to her energy and versatility.

Mrs Gold allowed me to ride Gay Gordon when he had retired so that I could perfect my flying change aids. This was of great help to me and I went on to train Desert Storm and Xenocles to Grand Prix level before I had that important ride on Kadett which I described in Chapter 1. It was with Kadett that I was lucky enough to be included in several teams with Mrs Johnstone, and also to ride in my first Olympics in Munich in 1972. My subsequent successes with Dutch Courage and his son Dutch Gold, together with those of my teammates, helped considerably to raise interest in the sport in Britain.

TODAY'S YOUNG STARS

Christopher Bartle's recent successes with Wily Trout — sixth in the 1984 Los Angeles Olympics and fourth in the European Championships in 1985 — gave British dressage a great boost. He then went on to come second in the first World Cup Musical Championships in 1986. His sister, Jane Bartle-Wilson, has also had major successes in international competitions, winning the Musical Freestyle at Goodwood and coming second in the same class at the World Championships in Toronto 1986, where I came a close third on my present Grand Prix horse, Dutch Gold. Perhaps the most exciting current aspect of British dressage is the strength of our Young Riders who in 1986 took the team Silver Medal in

(Left) **Jane Bartle-Wilson on Pinocchio** at Goodwood. This rider is a consistent performer in the British team, and she excels in musical freestyle competition.

(Right) **Dutch Courage** at Goodwood, England. This is the horse who has taught me the most. His personality, his athletic ability and his classical piaffe have made him a pleasure to train and ride.

(Previous page) Riders from the French School, the **Cadre Noir**, performing airs above the ground during one of their spectacular displays.

Kronberg, West Germany, beating thirteen teams of the same age.

In recent years, American riders have been able to work with American trainers, such as Michael Pulin. Pulin's rider, Lendon Grey, rode with Gwen Stockebrand and John Winnett in the Alternate Olympics in 1980.

Presently riding successfully for the US in the new World Cup Musical Competitions in Europe are Robert Dover and Sandy Pfluger-Clark. The first US representative to the World Cup Championships in 1986 was Diana Rankin with New Lady Killer.

THE FUTURE OF DRESSAGE

The Dressage Group of the British Horse Society was set up in 1961 with 123 members and eight competitions. The membership is now over 5,000 with more than 400 competitions and at least 3,000 registered horses competing. There can be no doubt that the continuing international successes of British horses and riders have contributed overwhelmingly to this growth.

Another major support for British dressage has been the keen interest shown by Lord and Lady March who have hosted international competitions at their lovely Sussex home, Goodwood House, since 1973. The facilities there are splendid, with superb stabling, lovely riding areas and two excellent permanent arenas all set in the beautiful grounds in front of the house. Goodwood House has now hosted the World Championships in 1978, the Alternative Olympics in 1980, and the European Championships in 1987, when the best riders in the world have competed.

Britain is now beginning to breed horses capable of taking part in world-class events, and it is now up to the riders and trainers to keep up with the rapidly growing international standards of the sport.

Three **Lipizzaners** from John Lassiter's school, performing a **pas de trois** to music. The riders are in period costume for this display.

DRESSAGE TO MUSIC

The advent of dressage to music has also had a considerable influence on the appeal of the sport throughout the world in recent years. It has really caught the imagination of the public, who are becoming increasingly aware of the equestrian art of movement in correspondence with rhythms and tonalities.

Of course, it is important that the sport does not become gimmicky, but there seems little likelihood of

this: riders are now preparing excellent programmes of movements well suited to their chosen music. Some riders are using classical music, and ride movements and changes of direction as the mood takes them, interpreting the music freely. Other riders choose popular music with a more emphatic beat. It is, perhaps, more difficult to keep the horse constantly on the beat, but it can be very effective when well ridden. With the World Cup Qualifiers and Championships to Music, we have seen capacity crowds clamouring for seats. Given such tremendous interest, it is vital that the performances are ones which the spectators will remember. The choreography and composition of the programme are very important, not only from the point of view of entertainment, but also because more difficult movements score higher points.

THE RULES OF MUSICAL DRESSAGE

There are freestyle tests to music from Novice standard right up to Grand Prix level, all with fixed lengths of time. For Novice standard it is four minutes, so it is advisable to keep your taped music about 15 seconds shorter than this to allow for the variation in the machines used at competitions. At each level, you are given set movements together with a list of options, and the rider must not show movements above his standard. The higher the standard, the more you can put into the programme, but all movements must be derived from classical dressage and never circusy, like cantering backwards, Spanish Walk, or pivoting on one leg. Classical 'Airs above the Ground' cannot be included either. Riding with the reins in one hand is allowed, when the free arm must be held at the rider's side. At all levels the salute must be given at halt on the centre line at the beginning and end of the test.

Before composing a programme, write to the Dressage Offices of the British Horse Society and ask for all the dressage-to-music score sheets. These will explain the requirements and scoring at each standard, and give extra movements to choose from which will help to make the programme more aesthetically pleasing. At Grand Prix level, the walk, either collected or extended, must be shown, together with collected trot including half-pass to right and left, extended trot, collected canter including half-pass right and left, extended canter, flying changes every second stride, and flying changes every stride. Pirouette right and left both earn double marks (a

coefficient mark), as do piaffe and passage. The judges like to see a well-patterned programme but it is a mistake to try to do a difficult programme when your horse is not ready for it. If harmony, lightness and ease of movement suffer, you will also lose points. You will get better marks if you do the required movements well. Naturally, though, you cannot expect to beat a rider who has a very advanced horse and can show double pirouettes, flying changes on the circle with the reins in one hand, piaffe straight and in pirouette, half-passes in passage and on the straight line with excellent transitions into and out of piaffe!

THE ARTISTIC CHALLENGE

Dressage to music can be really exciting to ride. As riders, we must constantly think up new ideas, and there have been increasingly artistic and inventive displays. Of course, we cannot put on a high-class performance unless we have been very dedicated and trained our horses so that they can perform with grace, lightness and in complete harmony with us. This is what most appeals to both judges and spectators, and is a most rewarding and satisfying challenge.

International trainers are getting together to discuss their ideas and training methods. The judges are still having some problems on fixing precise requirements in competition. However, I am sure we are now going to see such a rise in the standard of performance, and that the displays will be so accomplished, that the judging will become very straightforward. The real enthusiast comes to see the Grand Prix and to study both horse and rider in the quietness of the arena, but dressage to music has immense crowd appeal, and thousands of people are now coming to watch it. Sponsors are, of course, delighted with this particular aspect of the sport, for the dressage image of impulsion, strength, suppleness and elegance is marvellous for their advertising.

Dressage displays have helped to popularize the sport, especially amongst the young. It was Madame Liz Hartel's beautiful display to music in 1952 which first showed me that dressage was what I really wanted to do, as I described in Chapter 1.

It is important to remember that there are many elements to true horsemanship. Throughout my life I have enjoyed all sorts of riding, including show jumping, horse trials and point-to-pointing. I find they have all helped me in their different ways to understand speed and timing, so essential in all forms of riding. Even when teaching, I find that jumping helps to loosen the horse, giving him variety and the chance to get rid of his surplus energy.

THE AIM OF DRESSAGE

Dressage is a time-consuming and fascinating study and one which demands of its devotees the self-motivation and self-discipline to work the horse correctly and to work just as hard on their own position and aids. A good rider must constantly check himself. After all, a horse only goes as well as he is ridden.

During the everyday involvement of riding, training and competing, it is important that we never lose sight of the aim of dressage which is for horse and rider to achieve complete harmony with each other. A really fine, well-trained partnership is able to perform classical movements with the freedom, lightness and ease which make dressage such a pleasure to watch. This is the perfection we all strive for.

I hope, having read this far, that this book will help you to get as much pleasure from riding and training your horse as I have had over the years. My final tribute must be to the horses I have ridden who have taught me so much, and it is to them that I will always be eternally grateful.

(Opposite) The aim of dressage is well summed up in this picture. **Dutch Bid** portrays power and balance in perfect harmony.

GLOSSARY

Above the Bit When a horse raises its head and stretches forward with the neck, so that its mouth and the bit are above the rider's hand. This makes control difficult, and spoils the horse's outline and paces.

Affiliated Dressage Competitions Dressage competitions run by, or under the auspices of, the British Horse Society Dressage Group. To enter, horses must be registered with the British Horse Society, and they are awarded points dependent upon their placing in the competition. They are then graded according to the number of points they have amassed.

Aids Signals given by the rider to convey his wishes to the horse.

Aids, Artificial Whips, spurs and any form of martingale or third rein used by the rider.

Aids, Diagonal Combination of aids given with the hand and leg on opposite sides.

Aids, Lateral Combination of aids given with the hand and leg on the same side.

Aids, Natural The rider's seat, legs, hands, body and voice.

'Airs above the Ground' Advanced movements performed by horses trained in the art of *haute école* or high school. Horses trained in the art of dressage are not expected to perform these movements.

Back, To Stage in training a young horse when he is first introduced to having a rider on his back.

Balanced When in movement, the horse carries his own weight and that of his rider evenly, which allows him to perform all paces and movements smoothly and fluently. Balance depends to some extent on conformation, but a rider can help greatly in keeping a horse well balanced.

Breast Plate A leather strap which passes around the front of the horse's chest and is attached at either end to the roller (*see below*) or saddle, to keep them in place.

Canter A pace in three-time, in which one hind leg strikes off, followed by the other hind leg and diagonal foreleg moving together, and lastly the other foreleg. There is then a moment of suspension.

Canter, Collected Canter pace in which the steps are comparatively short and elevated, and the horse's outline somewhat compressed as a result.

Canter, Disunited Canter pace in which the sequence of steps is wrong, so that the leading foreleg and hind leg appear to be on the same side.

Canter, Extended Canter in which the steps are lengthened so as to cover as much ground as possible, whilst the pace remains controlled and balanced.

Canter, Left Canter in which the left or nearside foreleg appears to be leading the pace.

Canter, Medium Canter pace in which the steps are a little longer and less elevated than in the collected pace.

Canter, Right Canter in which the right or offside foreleg appears to be leading the pace.

Capriole One of the 'Airs above the ground'; the horse raises its forelegs off the ground with the hocks deeply bent, then jumps forward and, with the body horizontal, kicks out violently with the hind legs.

Cavesson Item of tack used in breaking or training a young horse. Similar to a strong leather headcollar in appearance, it has a padded noseband with three swivelling metal rings, to which the lunge or side reins are attached.

Cheek Snaffle Snaffle bit with long metal pieces extending above and below the rings at either end of the mouthpiece. These are kept in place by leather 'keepers' on the cheek pieces of the bridle. A good bit to use in training if the horse is inclined to fuss or to put his tongue over the bit.

Collection In movement, the horse is at his most agile, with the potential energy of a coiled spring, but no mental tension. His hind legs are well under him to give him maximum impulsion and his outline is shortened, allowing his steps to be higher and more mobile.

Corbette One of the 'Airs above the ground'; the horse assumes the *levade* position (*see below*), then takes a series of jumps forward on his hind legs — his forelegs remaining off the ground.

Counter Canter Canter round the manège or on a circle when the horse leads with the outside foreleg.

Counter Change of Hand A half-pass, performed from the centre line to the track and back to the centre line, or vice versa.

Double Bridle A bridle which has two bits — a snaffle and a curb. It allows an experienced rider the most refined degree of control, and its use is compulsory in certain dressage competitions.

Drop Noseband A noseband that buckles beneath the bit. It is used with a snaffle bridle and helps to prevent a horse opening its mouth or crossing its jaws to evade the action of the bit. Must be carefully adjusted.

Dutch Warmblood A breed of riding horse popular for dressage, or for breeding a potential dressage horse.

Extension In movement, the horse's length of stride is increased to its fullest extent, while the horse remains lightly on the bit, calm and attentive to the rider.

Fédération Equestre Internationale (FEI) Equestrian body which governs the sport of riding on an international competitive basis.

FEI Intermédiaire I Dressage test which comes between Prix St Georges and Intermédiaire II. It includes flying changes at every second stride and full canter pirouettes to the left and right.

FEI Intermédiaire II Dressage test which comes between Intermédiaire I and Grand Prix. It includes flying changes at every stride and a few steps of piaffe.

Flash Noseband A combination of an ordinary cavesson noseband and a drop noseband. Useful for keeping the bit very stable in a horse's mouth.

Flexion Of the head, when the head is bent at the poll without showing tension or strain, and while keeping the jaw relaxed. Of the body or neck, indicating a very slight bend in a required direction.

Flying Change In canter when, at the rider's request, the horse jumps from one canter leading leg to the other, during the moment of suspension in the pace.

Goodwood House The Sussex home of Lord and Lady March, and the annual venue of the best known competitive dressage events in Great Britain. The World Championships, the Alternative Olympics and the European Championships have all taken place at Goodwood since competitions began there in 1973.

Grand Prix Most advanced of the FEI's dressage tests; movements required include passage, piaffe, flying changes at every stride, and pirouettes at canter, as well as all the school paces.

Half-halt A slight checking of the movement, requested by the rider in any pace to make the horse attentive, and alert him to the fact that he is about to be given a specific new instruction.

Half-pass A forward and sideways movement on two tracks, in which the horse is very slightly bent through the length of his body in the direction in which he is going. Half-pass may be performed in walk, trot or canter.

Half-pirouette A 180° turn, in which the horse steps around the inside hind leg without stopping, his body flexed in the direction of the movement. Usually performed at the walk or canter.

Hanoverian A German breed of horse with strong bone conformation much favoured by dressage riders.

Haute Ecole The classical art of riding and training, following the traditions of the great European riding masters of bygone centuries. In its highest form it covers the 'Airs above the ground' (*see above*), generally only practised nowadays by horses and riders from the Spanish Riding School in Vienna.

Holstein Another German breed of riding horse favoured by dressage riders.

Impulsion The forward surge of movement in a horse that comes from the energetic use of the hocks and gives spring and energy to all paces. Impulsion is created by the rider using his legs and seat, and it should be controlled and regulated by the hands.

Lateral Work Movements in which the horse moves forwards and sideways, his feet moving on two tracks.

Leg Yielding Sideways movements in which the horse moves away from the rider's leg aid. The horse should remain straight in the body, except for a very slight inclination away from the direction in which he is travelling.

Levade One of the 'Airs above the ground'; the horse raises its forehand off the ground, bending its forelegs, and remains motionless, its hind legs deeply bent.

Lipizzaner A breed descended from the Arab Barb and Andalusian horses. Stallions of the breed are used by riders at the Spanish Riding School of Vienna to perform the movements of *haute école*.

Long-reining The training of a young horse, in which the trainer controls him from the ground by the use of long reins. These are attached to the rings on either side of the cavesson and led through rings on the breaking roller.

Loose-ring Snaffle Snaffle bit in which the rings can move round in their position at either end of the mouthpiece. A lightweight, loose-ring snaffle is a good bit to use when beginning the training of a horse.

Lunge Rein A single webbing rein, usually about 7.6 metres (25 ft) long, attached to the central ring of the cavesson noseband and held by the trainer as he directs the horse around him on a circle during training.

Manège A rectangular schooling area for training horse and rider. A manège or arena used for dressage will either be 40×20 metres, or 60×20 metres, the larger size being used for the more advanced tests. Both arenas are marked with letters, placed at intervals around the outside. 'X' marks the centre of the manège.

Musical Freestyle Dressage tests from Novice up to Grand Prix level of a fixed length of time, in which the rider plans his or her own test, to a piece of music of his or her choice. At each level, the tests have set movements which must be performed, as well as a list of options.

Overtracking When the prints made by the hind feet fall in front of those made by the forefeet in the stride. In extended paces, the hind feet should overtrack to the maximum.

Pacing A fault at walk when the pace becomes two-time, as the near and offside legs move together laterally. The horse usually stiffens his back and raises his head.

Passage An advanced dressage movement in which the horse springs forward in a very slow, cadenced trot, the moment of suspension being increased by the high, slowly executed steps.

Piaffe An advanced dressage movement in which the horse remains on the spot, lifting his legs in two-time in a springy, cadenced trot.

Pirouette A 360° turn, executed in walk, piaffe or canter. The horse executes the circle in one fluent movement without stopping, and the diameter of the circle should be approximately equal to the horse's length.

Port An upward indentation in the centre of the mouthpiece of a curb bit, to allow more room for the horse's tongue. Ports can be of varying depths.

Prix St Georges The most elementary of the FEI's *haute école* tests. Medium, collected and extended paces have to be performed, together with half-passes, flying changes at every third stride, and half-pirouettes at the canter.

Rein-back An active movement backwards in two-time; diagonal fore and hind legs move together.

Renvers A lateral movement performed on two tracks, in which the hind legs remain on the track and the forelegs are brought inwards on to a separate, but overlapping track.

Roller Strong girth, strapped round a horse's middle before the saddle is used, during early lunge training. Small rings on either side are for side or long reins. It should be held in place by a breast-plate.

Schaukel An advanced rein-back movement, in which the horse walks back correctly for a fixed number of steps, immediately walks forward for a set number of steps, and then back again for another fixed sequence of steps.

Self-carriage The natural carriage of a horse without interference from the rider. Combined with correct balance, it allows for the best performance of paces.

Serpentine A series of half-circles of the same size, performed in opposite directions one after the other down the length of the arena. Used in training a horse to supple him on curves and teach obedience.

Side Reins Short reins attached to the side rings of the cavesson, or to the rings of a bit at one end and to the rings of the breaking roller or saddle at the other. Used in training on the lunge to help with correct head carriage.

Simple Change The change of leading legs at the canter, executed by bringing the horse back to walk or trot for a few strides before asking him to strike off on the new lead.

Shoulder-fore One of the lateral movements used early in training, in which the shoulder is brought in from the track of the inside hind leg. As with leg-yielding, the horse is taught to move away from the rider's leg aid.

Shoulder-in A similar movement to shoulder-fore, but it requires more bend and collection from the horse. The hind legs remain on the original track and the forelegs are brought inwards onto a separate, parallel, but overlapping track. The horse is bent away from the direction of movement.

Tail-coat Close-fitting coat with tails, worn by riders competing in all advanced dressage tests.

Tempo Changes Flying changes of leg, executed every set number of strides, from every stride to every second, third or fourth stride.

Trakhener A breed of riding horse much used in the breeding of dressage horses, especially to lighten some of the European warmblood breeds.

Transition A change of pace upwards, from walk to trot to canter, or downwards. Also a change within a pace, as from collected to medium to extended trot, or vice versa.

Travers A lateral movement performed on two tracks, in which the forehand remains on the track while the hind legs are brought inwards onto a separate, parallel, but overlapping track. The horse is bent round the rider's inside leg, his head and neck slightly flexed in the direction of the movement.

Trot A pace in two-time, in which the legs move actively in diagonal pairs.

Trot, Collected Trot, Extended Trot, Medium Trots in which the definition of the steps and movement follows the same requirements as in collected, extended or medium canters (*see above*).

Turn on the Forehand A pivoting movement, in which the horse moves his hind legs round in a half-circle or full circle, with one foreleg acting as the pivot.

Walk A pace in four-time, in which each foot comes to the ground separately but with regularity.

Walk, Collected Walk, Extended Walk, Medium Walks in which the definition of the steps and movement follows the same requirements as in collected, extended or medium canters (*see above*).

Wolf Teeth Rudimentary teeth, found just in front of the molars, usually only on the upper jaw. If they have sharp points, they can cause pain when the cavesson is firmly adjusted round the nose.

Zigzag Half-passes A series of half-passes of a set number of steps, performed to either side of the centre line of the arena or manège.

INDEX

ACKNOWLEDGMENT

The Novice and Grand Prix Dressage Tests on page 129 are reproduced by permission of the British Horse Society and the Fédération Equestre Internationale.